Masha Ibeschitz

Impact

Masha Ibeschitz

Impact

**Develop Your People –
Enhance Your Company's Success**

WILEY

WILEY-VCH Verlag GmbH & Co. KGaA

All books published by **Wiley-VCH** are carefully produced. Nevertheless, authors, editors, and publisher do not warrant the information contained in these books, including this book, to be free of errors. Readers are advised to keep in mind that statements, data, illustrations, procedural details or other items may inadvertently be inaccurate.

© **2018 Wiley-VCH Verlag & Co. KGaA, Boschstr. 12, 69469 Weinheim, Germany**

All rights reserved (including those of translation into other languages). No part of this book may be reproduced in any form – by photoprinting, microfilm, or any other means – nor transmitted or translated into a machine language without written permission from the publishers. Registered names, trademarks, etc. used in this book, even when not specifically marked as such, are not to be considered unprotected by law.

Library of Congress Card No.:

applied for

British Library Cataloguing-in-Publication Data

A catalogue record for this book is available from the British Library.

English version by Jutta Scherer and Ann-Terry Gilman (Munich and Duesseldorf, Germany)

Figures were created by visual solutions, Mag. Christoph J. Tamussino und Löwenherz, Mag. Martina Gräser.

Bibliographic information published by the Deutsche Nationalbibliothek

The Deutsche Nationalbibliothek lists this publication in the Deutsche Nationalbibliografie; detailed bibliographic data are available on the Internet at <http://dnb.d-nb.de>.

Printed in the Federal Republic of Germany
Printed on acid-free paper

Gestaltung: pp030 – Produktionsbüro Heike Praetor, Berlin
Cover: Torge Stoffers, Leipzig
Coverfoto: tiero - stock.adobe.com
Satz: Lumina Datamatics
Druck & Bindung: CPI books GmbH, Leck

Print ISBN: 978-3-527-50966-9
ePub ISBN: 978-3-527-82205-8

10 9 8 7 6 5 4 3 2 1

Contents

Foreword		9
Introduction	Why managers should also be development guides	11

If you use coaching tools to give people impetus – that is, inspire and motivate them to develop their potential – you can strengthen the whole organization while dedicating more time and energy to the strategic management of your business. This book shows you how.

Chapter 1	The strategy dilemma – or: How to make time for your priorities	15

If you neglect strategic tasks today, they will hit you in the face tomorrow – and more so in the VUCA world. Here are some ideas for new solutions.

Chapter 2	Engaging your staff through communication – or: Please use the elevator!	31

To trigger a certain response, you need to engage people. It helps to have a basic understanding of different personality types – and to know the corresponding approaches.

Chapter 3	How to increase value contributions – or: The blessings of coaching	47

Every individual has hidden potential. Coaching is one way to develop that potential and increase a person's value contributions.

Chapter 4	Coaching occasions – or: Can I actually do something myself?	63

The coaching toolbox is big and colorful. If you know the basics, you can provide people with valuable impetus in many situations. This may accomplishmuch more than traditional people development events.

Chapter 5	**Helping people help themselves – or: Just ask the right questions**	79
	If you know what approaches are appropriate in which situations, you can choose among them dynamically – almost as though you were moving a slider. That is a key part of agile leadership.	
Chapter 6	**Who is coachable? – or: You can't make pigs fly**	95
	Everyone is coachable, but not in every situation. Appropriate skills and resources are key for people to help themselves – after they've been given the appropriate impetus.	
Chapter 7	**Making coaching possible – or: Proper tool application is key**	109
	A development guide always makes sure to create the right setting for conversations with employees. Trust is the basis; questions help establish clarity.	
Chapter 8	**Finding solutions – or: When people don't know what they know**	125
	If you assume people know more than they are aware of, you can help them solve their own problems – with courage and creativity.	
Chapter 9	**Tools and techniques – or: No matter what I use, it will work!**	141
	Helpful tools and techniques abound – and it doesn't really matter which ones you choose. What matters much more is your attitude: the key is to switch from "telling" to "asking."	
Chapter 10	**Problem-solving in all directions – or: Back to the future**	159
	Agile problem-solving considers the past, the present, and the future – each as thoroughly as needed in any given situation. The focus is on what people agree on as the desired future state of things.	
Closing remarks		**175**
Further reading		**177**

Contents

Thanks! 179
About the author 181
Index 183

Foreword

Coaching is a live issue for many organisations. A significant number amongst those would lay claim to a 'coaching culture'. Despite this profession of a developmentally focused organisation with managers who spend time building the capability and competence of their people, few have the kind of clarity to develop coaching behaviours amongst those who manage people.

One of the challenges is to ensure that there is a common understanding and language around what the expected activity might be and shared expectations about the role of those who lead teams of people. Ask nine managers in an organisation with a clear commitment to a coaching culture and you may find ten different definitions of what coaching is and what it is not!

The focus of Masha Ibeschitz's book is to tell stories. Stories which illuminate and resonate. Stories which describe the over-operationally involved role of many modern managers. Stories which shed light on those difficult or unsatisfactory conversations when – despite the best intentions – problems remain and unhelpful behaviours are unchanged. She also shows how those conversations can succeed, by using pragmatic coaching tools.

Masha's approach is to be extremely clear about what coaching is and – perhaps most importantly – what it isn't. If nothing else, those who read this book will come away with clear definitions. Through her storytelling, she illuminates the issues which can hinder as well as the tools which can promote effective coaching conversations. Each chapter ends with a brief list of key takeaways; bullet point summaries which inform of changed practice.

Not every organisation is structured to facilitate the kind of coaching exchange which Masha advocates yet. It would be great if sometimes leaders were enabled – and given the time – to lead. Perhaps the greatest contribution 'Impact' can make is on those in the upper echelons of organisations who blithely talk about team leaders coaching their people while erecting insuperable barriers to them ever being able to fulfil this portion of their role. Through an appreciation of the possibilities of implementing effective coaching and choosing tools wisely, it is devoutly to be hoped that management can move from being a status to being an activity – an activity focused on enabling people to give of their best and enhance the organisations' success.

Robin Hoyle, FLPI

Introduction
Why managers should also be development guides

Does your work diary look like a big, colorful patchwork rug? Does checking your emails feel like someone has opened the floodgates? Are you wondering whether you will ever find the time you need to devote to your strategic work? This book is for you.

In the following chapters, I will show you how you can use certain coaching techniques to develop your people so they can support you more effectively and you can work jointly towards your company's success. Developing your people to a sufficient level is essential for you to be able to rely on them fully. Key tasks can and should be delegated only to truly capable and engaged people – I assume you agree. Employees who haven't been developed to the level required can turn into nuisances. They'll take up much of your time and attention by keeping you tied down with everyday chores. Tasks you delegated will come boomeranging back. In the end, you'll face destructive stress patterns, preventing you and your organization from enjoying the fruits of your work.

It doesn't have to be like this.

Once you master a few basic skills of coaching, you'll take a crucial step: from being a manager to being a leader and development guide for your people. You'll be able to give them exactly the impetus they need for their development and which fits their current situation. Both sides will benefit, and so will the overall system and thus your company. Everyday business offers countless opportunities to use coaching techniques productively. These include situations that might not call for coaching at first: You want to ensure that a creative brainstorming session produces good results? There are techniques for that. Resolve a conflict between two wranglers? Not a big challenge for someone who has mastered coaching techniques. Once you've started using the tools in the big and colorful coaching toolbox, you'll know how to give the right kind of impetus for each and every situation – in your role as a development guide.

I have long been mulling over the idea of providing managers with a kind of vade-mecum, a quick and easy guide to learning the basics of coaching. Now I've finally found the necessary inspiration and patience – and the right professional support – to make it happen. This book is not intended as a replacement for any of the training programs for coaches, or for any of the specialized coaching literature. Experience has taught me, however, that getting the full training as a coach is usually out of the question for many managers, due to time restraints – or at least they won't be able to make it any time soon. This book will provide everyone who leads people on a daily basis with a "best of coaching" collection, for immediate use in your daily management practice.

In writing this book, I have drawn on over 20 years of coaching experience, which I've gathered in the international business environment and with companies of virtually all sizes and in a wide array of industries – as both a coach and a coachee. Be assured that I've personally experienced each of the situations described here from a 360° perspective. You can also be sure that none of these situations took place exactly as described. If, for instance, you read about a male CEO of a large Italian-based furniture company, there's a 50% chance that this person really was a man. It may have been a woman. And you can be fairly certain the individual was neither Italian nor in the furniture industry. In other words, I have taken great care to choose real events and disguise them thoroughly by shifting them to other locations and industries, changing the backdrops such as hotels or convention centers, and, of course, giving everyone fantasy names. I did place my stories mostly in Europe, which does not mean they may not have happened elsewhere. As a world citizen with an Austrian passport, I've taken the liberty to immortalize my home country, so to speak, by making it the occasional venue of a story. There may not be much to be said for it, but there is nothing to be said against it, either – right?

Finally, a stern warning: This book contains humor. The observations I am sharing with you come with a twinkle in my eye. Not to be mistaken for irony or sarcasm, mind you. When I look at human weaknesses, challenges, and coaching needs with a sense of humor, it is out of love for human nature and my experience that it makes learning easier. So, you may find some of the stories in this book to be slightly exaggerated. I also take the liberty of playing occasionally with gender stereotypes, sprinkling them with humor or even reversing them. That said, it is always possible that a detail you believe must be pure fiction is actually true. Fact is stranger than fiction, they say.

If you are now wondering whether this book is all fiction: No, it's not. But storytelling is a great tool that helps depict complex situations in ways that make them easier to grasp and keep in mind. At the factual level, I always try to be as concise as possible and as comprehensive as necessary when I give you the key takeaways that will help you become a development guide for your staff. Each chapter begins with a brief overview and ends with a summary. Where appropriate, special topics are addressed in separate text boxes. You'll get the most out of this book if you read the chapters sequentially, as they build one on the next. Later on, perhaps you will want to revisit specific topics.

I really hope that this book will help you increase your impact and make a tangible difference – for yourself, your staff, and your organization.

Sincerely,
Masha Ibeschitz

Chapter 1
The strategy dilemma – or:
How to make time for your priorities

Too little time for strategic management tasks? Tell me something new. It seems to be a problem most managers have – and it goes back many years. The odds are, it won't get better on its own. On the contrary: In times where everything happens at once and new developments keep catching us by surprise, the pressure is likely to keep rising. If you can't make enough time for essential things today, chances are you'll find even less time tomorrow. Unless you revisit your own attitude. You might discover a trick that miraculously helps you free up some space for your strategic tasks.

"What's that you just said? What about the machine?" Frank was suddenly all ears. The strategy meeting with the regional directors at his company, a global rubber manufacturer, had been going on for 10 minutes. And just a second ago, someone had mentioned a machine failure at a plant in Slovenia. Frank – in his late forties, former head of the company's German operations, then US operations, now Director Western & Central Europe, wanted all the details. His look was that of a family father whose eleven-year-old is casually telling him over dinner that he's set a wildfire in the woods that is now spreading towards town. "How is it even possible for a machine that was just delivered to be down for days and stall our whole production?" he rumbled.

Helen, Director of the Americas, merely glanced at him as if to say, "So what? Shit happens." Having grown up on a farm in South Africa, she was not easily shaken and very pragmatic. Not so Peter, the Regional Head of Eastern Europe. He immediately leaped at this chance to demonstrate his engineering savvy. A heated discussion ensued. Sooner or later, everyone else took out their smartphones and started checking emails – except for Helen, who was watching Peter and Frank stoically. At some point, she drily told them: "By the way, guys: lunch with Ricarda's on in 20 minutes."

Ricarda was the company CEO – had been in that role for a year now, previously CFO – so all the regional directors reported to her. Knowing her, she would want an oral report on the results of their strategy meeting. Which, in her case, meant she would ask question after question and expect succinct, to-the-point answers. Before Frank left the room for lunch, he briefly checked his smartphone. Three calls from his wife – it was breakfast time in the US. They urgently needed to make a decision on whether or not to move his family back to Germany. A decision that wasn't easy, given that his kids thought their US high school was the coolest place on earth. "Well, Frank," he heard Helen mutter behind him, "this certainly felt like one pointless meeting. We know everything about the machines in Slovenia now, but do we have a strategy?"

The hamster wheel is spinning faster

Frank is a fictional character. As is the case for all other characters in this book, he has a different name in real life, and he does not work for a rubber manufacturer. His situation, however, is very real – and similar to problems countless other top managers face. They use coaching services because they realize things are getting worse, and they can't seem to find a solution. The hustle and bustle of everyday operations is eating up their time. At the same time, they fully realize that with each step on the career ladder, they have assumed more and more responsibility for the greater whole, which means they cannot allow themselves to get caught up in operational details. None of the managers I've met needed a coach to tell them they should schedule more time for strategic tasks. That's what people in management functions are supposed to do. They're expected to determine financial and culture-related targets, and to set the course for higher revenues and necessary change. They need a mission and vision that is up to date at all times, and they need a plan for how to turn this mission and vision into reality in their organization. All of this is widely known. Yet, at the end of the day, managers often find they just don't have enough time. Their focus is on operational, not strategic issues. As one senior executive put it: "With top managers and strategy, it's often like with teenagers and sex: they talk about it constantly, but rarely ever get down to business."

Welcome to a world where nothing is as it used to be

So this is what I call the strategy dilemma: Every manager knows that strategy and targets are top priorities. But in practice that's what they spend the least amount of time on. Nothing new here, you may say, we've all been facing this problem for years. And you are right. What's new is that this dilemma has disastrous consequences in a growing number of cases, as the external business environment is undergoing a fundamental change. I am talking about the VUCA world. Oh dear – VUCA, you think. Yes, I know. A buzzword, if there ever was one. An acronym you come across on a daily basis. Believe me, I would like to spare you – if only there wasn't so much truth in it.

Everyone is talking about VUCA – but what is it really about? Before you start googling, here's what the four letters stand for: *volatility, uncertainty, complexity,* and *ambiguity.* In these times of digitalization and rampant globalization, the world is becoming less and less steady. There's an increasing level of risk and complexity. And, as if that weren't enough, we're also living in an era of ambiguity: Clear answers are few and far between, everything is "this … *and* this, too." (See the text box "Are you ready for VUCA ?")

Are you ready for VUCA?

Everything is in flux, nothing is permanent, and the next crisis is always looming. Products and services are getting more and more complex. Artificial intelligence is advancing. Situations and pieces of information can be read in various ways. Fake news and post-factual narratives add to the fogginess. That's the VUCA environment for you. Here's some good news, though: In your position, you are free to choose how to deal with it. If you choose acceptance, it will surely be for your own good.

Go ahead and accept volatility, uncertainty, complexity, and ambiguity as factors you can't change anyway. Adopt a positive stance – then you'll be able to embrace VUCA as an opportunity and move to a new level of leadership. It will also enable you to leave yesterday's success formulas and linear thinking behind you. So what if the world is no longer black or white, one or zero? Deal with it productively. Embrace flexibility, aliveness, and openness – then you'll be able to transform the VUCA world into something you can shape. Practice alchemy!

These are the possible outcomes:

- Volatility becomes Vision.
- Uncertainty becomes Understanding.
- Complexity becomes Clarity.
- Ambiguity becomes Agility.

Give a meaning to chaos. Develop bold visions. Open your mind, change your perspective, look for new, holistic forms of knowledge. Understand situations by recognizing the underlying patterns, and call things by their real names. Communicate clearly. Expand your network and trust in its power. Decide and act quickly. Reduce hierarchy in your company. Keep your eyes on the big picture, and take responsibility for wrong decisions. If you do all these things, the VUCA world will become the best of all worlds. Pluck up your courage, and distinguish yourself from managers who merely react to things instead of shaping them.

What has gotten us here won't get us any further

The VUCA world presents leaders with new challenges – not only in management but also in their personal lives. Roles and positions keep changing faster and faster. Frank, for instance, feels as though he's only just moved to the US with his family, and now is expected to come back to Germany to take on a new role at headquarters. All of a sudden, he's in charge of over 30 countries, and he wonders where the best place is to move his family so he'll be able to see them every once in a while.

All of this wouldn't be such a problem if people could only adapt as fast as the world changes. Well, they can't, and that makes things difficult. In Austria, my home country, when a man buys a "janker" – a traditional jacket made of loden, a boiled-wool fabric – it never fits at first. It takes quite a while for the loden to soften and adjust to the wearer's body. It's similar with today's generation of managers and the external environment. In most cases, a manager's internal world has not adjusted to the external one. The prevailing sentiment is: What has gotten me this far will also get me further. It's been like that for so many years. So, usually, managers will accept any offer to move further up the ladder. Only very few stop to wonder whether they are really the right person for the new role, given their specific skills, attitudes, and ways of tackling their everyday tasks. Alright, they say instead, so I have even greater responsibilities and will have to deliver on them. Until the situation escalates. That's what happened to Frank. And that's what has happened to many of the people I've met in my role as a top executive coach.

Door number one or door number two?

Frank was back at his company's headquarters on the outskirts of a southern German town, which was fairly well-known but not an attraction. Here, where urban infrastructure was thinning, streets were wide and truck traffic heavy, he was working out of a fairly nice-looking high-rise building, with simple and functional interior decor. The term "Hidden Champions" was not very popular on the executive floors – mostly due to the "hidden" part, while the "champion" part was deemed fitting. For years, the company had considered itself a global player with humble roots. Here, Frank and his fellow managers were sitting with the CEO one day after lunch. Frank hadn't been able to enjoy the food for even a minute. Instead of the superfood salad topped with quinoa, nuts, and an agave-based vinaigrette, he was sorely craving a juicy burger with extra ketchup and mayonnaise. But eating a heavy meal like that would have looked like refusing to perform. And while Ricarda was talking about her 9-day hiking tour through the Nepalese Annapurna massif, Frank's wife bombarded him with WhatsApp messages, quoting verbatim what their kids had to say about the imminent loss of their new-found American friends. To Frank, being in the conference room was almost a relief. But the feeling didn't last.

As always, Ricarda asked for a summary of key findings. It didn't take her long to notice that her people hadn't gotten far in their effort to work out a digitalization strategy for the company. After giving them an irritated look, she demanded to know which of the key prerequisites for digitalization were currently met. "Let's take your production sites, Frank," Ricarda said, wanting to see some figures at least. "What's the percentage of processes at your plants for which we have real-time data?" Frank's head was spinning. His first thought was: I don't have a clue. His second: That's unfair – I've only been made Regional Director a few weeks ago. But of course he didn't say any of that. Instead, he muttered, "I'll look into it first thing in the morning. I'll have the numbers for you by the end of the week."

Ricarda didn't like hearing this. "Frank," she said calmly, looking him in the eye, "I am asking you this because we agreed a while ago to collect this data for each of our plants. I thought it had long since been done. I thought you guys had discussed our digital strategy on that basis this morning." Between the lines, Frank was hearing something else: "You are incompetent and unfit for your job. We should never have made you Regional Director; you're useless!" In response to these accusations – which only he had heard and Ricarda had never made – Frank now implored her, visibly upset: "I've got a 15-year track record of success at this company. All I'm asking for is a few days. Just give me a few days! I'll take care of this and get those numbers back to you by the end of the week." And while Frank's fellow managers remained silent, with a look of "Thank God it's him, not me" on their faces, the CEO finally said, "Alright, Frank. Thursday afternoon."

In his limousine to the Munich airport, Frank felt deeply frustrated as he thought about the meeting. He had planned to spend his night flight to Charlotte, North Carolina, working out a solution for his family problem. Now he urgently needed to look into digital process optimization. If he was lucky, the airport bookstore would have some specialized literature so he could read up on the subject.

Predictable responses under predictable conditions

Frank's reaction in the meeting with his CEO, Ricarda, is the result of a stress pattern that's quite common these days. Due to a chronic lack of time, managers are poorly sorted in terms of strategy and, as a result, feel overtaxed by the stream of new developments and requirements. Their to-do stack keeps piling up higher and higher, both at work and in their personal lives. In a situation like that, when colleagues, superiors, or customers confront you personally, it's a massive blow to your ego. As the US management trainer and systems theory expert Barry Oshry has put it, a reaction pattern like Frank's is a "predictable reflex responseunder predictable conditions." The system-immanent condition today is that top managers are overburdened. Their reflexive response, Oshry argues, is to continue doing what they have been doing and to keep absorbing more and more responsibility. That's what Frank is doing. Without a moment's hesitation, he signals to his boss: Yes, I'll take care of it, no problem. I'll get it done. It's a reflex – his acquired response to an accustomed stress pattern. Managers have always been under stress. But these days, in the VUCA environment, total overload has become almost standard for top executives. As a consequence, more and more individuals in management positions feel disempowered. Their health is at risk, their effectiveness dwindles, their personal lives suffer. At the end of the day, the question is: How much value can a chronically overburdened executive really contribute to his or her organization?

Do I wish to continue as before – or not?

We can't always change the systemic conditions we live in. What we *can* change is our inner attitude. Once I realize how certain conditions trigger certain reflex responses in me, I can stop to think about whether that is what I really want. If I know, for instance, that I find it hard to walk by an ice cream parlor without stopping to indulge, I can ask myself: Do I want to be this person who is conditioned that way – or do I want to be a person who decides on my own whether and when to treat myself to an ice cream? As trivial as this may sound, it isn't. The moment I switch to the mode of observer of my own behavior, I have begun breaking the pattern.

There are always two doors in life. Choosing the first means you'll continue acting the same way as before. Predictable conditions will trigger reflex responses. As a top manager, you will keep absorbing more and more responsibility – up to the point where you can't go on. Choosing the second door means you wake up, adopt a new stance, and practice real leadership. Once you've gone through the second door, you may realize that there are other people around you, so you don't have to do everything on your own. This may not sound like such a big surprise – but look at what happens in practice. How many top managers out there are able to sleep soundly every night, knowing they can rely on their people to keep things going?

Mission possible

For years, Mark had had no trouble sleeping. Now those days were over. In his mid-thirties, Mark had made a classic sales career at a leading consumer goods company. Selling was his forte, along with leading and motivating other sales people. In his sales organization, this set of strengths practically guaranteed a successful career. On top of that, Mark had held several overseas positions that had taken him from South America to Africa to the Persian Gulf, giving him ample opportunity to prove his ability to cope with pressure and to connect with people from different cultures. As traveling was one of his passions and he had no wife or children, he was more than delighted when the Luxembourg-based corporate headquarters promoted him to Sales Director for Western Asia, Africa, and the Middle East. A few months into the new job, his boss, the COO Sales and Marketing, invited him to a one-on-one talk at a hotel in Cologne, Germany.

"Look, Mark," he said, leaning forward in his leather armchair. "We're having problems in Pakistan. You've seen the country report. Rebel groups are taking over control of the transit routes in the mountains, and the government troops are no longer able to guarantee the safety of our transports. So, what we need to do is talk to the rebels and make a deal. That is, *you* will talk to them. You're the man, you can do it." After that conversation, Mark's thoughts were reeling. He imagined bearded men with machine guns pushing him into a tent, where he had to kneel before their leader and listen to his demands. Weapons, virgin slaves, Rolex watches, German SUVs. For two nights, Mark didn't sleep a wink. The third night, he had a dream in which he was forced at gun point to witness a decapitation. He started thinking about quitting the firm. What the management board was asking of him seemed like "Mission: Impossible." He had learned how to sell, how to set up a sales organization, and yes, he could do that anywhere in the world. But what made them think they could use him as a negotiator with terrorists?

On the morning of day four, Mark was creeping down the hallway to his office as if through a black tunnel, when Mike, a colleague, called his name from the coffee machine. In his early forties, Mike was an excellent salesman and one of the most unconventional types he had met. He drove a Harley, sported cowboy boots with his suit, and wore his hair tied into a small ponytail. There was hardly a country around the globe that Mike had not been to. "Man, you look like sh*t," he grinned, "What's going on?" Mike was always blunt like that, which could be a blessing sometimes. Mark felt a wave of relief. Finally, someone he could talk to! He told Mike about the meeting with his boss and the horror scenarios he had been imagining. Mike listened, then burst out laughing – and the longer Mark talked, the more Mike laughed. Finally, he said, "Calm down, buddy. No need to panic. I've been to Pakistan several times, even to rebel territory. It's true, they never put away their guns, they're almost like smartphones to them. But hospitality is a key value to them, a matter of honor. They'll do anything to prevent you from getting harmed, and you won't have a problem talking to them, either. As a matter of fact, if it's alright with you and Roger, I can come along. I like the country, the culture, and the cordiality the Pakistani people show you – conflict or not."

Every successful manager has strong people to support him or her

Many of the managers that hire me as a coach or reflection guide have forgotten one simple fact: That they are surrounded by people who are willing to help and would also be able to help, if they were only empowered. These managers accept every challenge and make the best of every situation – but they seem to think they have to do it all alone. When I ask them about this, they often ask me: "But what can I ask my people to do?" Or they say something like, "I'd really love to delegate stuff, but they won't do this as well as I can, so in the end it will all hit me in the back." Well, the truth is: Leaders need strong, capable people to support them. When a team manager is also the team's best expert, something's very wrong. Not always do we meet just the right people at just the right moment – as Mark did when he ran into Mike at the peak of his crisis – but even these coincidences happen more often than many managers realize.

When you want capable staff for your team, you usually have two options: Hire third parties – for good money – or develop them yourself. Unfortunately, recruiting good people is becoming increasingly difficult, as the war for talent is in full swing: Competing with big names like Apple or Google can be a big challenge for organizations. So, developing your own people is the better option.

You always attract people who are like you

The composition of your team may be the result of a series of coincidences. But it's not all coincidence: Unknowingly, we often attract people who are similar to ourselves. Have you ever seen photographs of business teams that made you think, hey, everyone looks more or less the same – faces, outfits, poses? That's one manifestation of the effect I'm talking about.

In organizations, as in life itself, nothing is static. Everything is in motion. As a leader you have the possibility to change things – yourself, your staff, and the system in your circle of influence – and to set the course for what kind of people you want around you in the future. If you think it might be an attractive option to develop yourself and your people, you will need an energy source. And you will need tools and techniques that work. The stronger your people are and the further developed, the better they can support you. And the more your people can contribute to your success, based on their unique personalities and capabilities, the less time you will need to invest in the day-to-day operations, and the more you can dedicate yourself to strategic management tasks. Sounds logical, doesn't it? So, one of the best ways to respond to the VUCA world is to have capable people – people who support their leaders in fulfilling the company's mission and meeting its financial targets.

Increase in effectiveness

"Long-distance flight, huh?" Philip couldn't resist commenting when he ran into another patron at the airport book store. Frank, with four books on his arm and two more squeezed between his knees, was leafing through book number seven. He briefly gazed at the younger man standing by the shelf. Philip was dressed casually but in style. Instead of a heavy briefcase, like the one Frank used to take on his flights, he carried a shoulder bag from a hip brand. At the moment, he was leafing through a booklet that looked a little like a children's book but seemed to be about a business topic. Something about mice. Or was it penguins? Frank hated it when strangers wanted to chat. But something about the younger man was different and made him want to continue the conversation. Perhaps it was his calm facial expression. Or his upright, energetic yet relaxed posture.

So, instead of doing the usual, and ignoring both the comment and its source, he replied: "Yeah, I'm taking the night flight to Charlotte. With a touch-down in Paris, unfortunately. The only direct flights leave around mid-day."

"Well, if you plan to read all those books on this trip, you better fly through Hong Kong," the man grinned.

Frank instantly regretted having said anything. This guy was a bit too sarcastic for his taste. Time for a retort: "Well, the comic book you have there probably won't take longer than the bus to the runway."

"Oh, it's not a comic book," Philip said with a wider grin, "it's the latest by Han H. Hirshberg – you know: the coaching and management guru. Best-selling author, too. The man's a genius! Truly masters the art of getting to the point in one sentence. His books are totally inspiring."

"Is that right." Frank found Philip's enthusiasm for a little book full of bright pictures somewhat odd. "Well, to each his own. I don't have time for coaching and things like that. I need to work on my company's digitalization strategy."

"And so you're trying to learn everything you can about the subject, right? Sounds familiar. I used to be like that myself. When I was Country Manager in Spain, I kept calling my Regional Director, who would then walk me through every little step I was to take. Until one day he got tired of it and asked his coach for advice. She told him to coach me instead of spoon-feeding me every little detail. Today I'm in charge of Western Europe, and I coach my people, too."

"Well, if I ever feel one of my people needs coaching, I'll find him a coach. I can't waste years of my life coaching my staff. I've got enough on my plate as it is."

"Oh, but you can use coaching tools as a manager. You don't need specific training for that, just common sense. That's what my former boss learned from his coach, and I then learned from him. Han H. Hirshberg writes about it, too."

"Let me see that rabbit book," Frank said, setting down his seven business books on a table where travel guides were displayed.

A fast and powerful lever for developing your staff

If you want to develop your people so that they can support you effectively and give you more time for the essential things, you have a number of options. Coaching is one of them. Because coaching is fast and powerful, it is ideal for the VUCA world. Over the past decades, coaching professionals and academics have generated a large toolbox with lots of tools that start getting results immediately. Managers can use them to trigger certain processes in people. Of course, learning to use a few tools can never replace professional training. But it simply wouldn't make sense for everyone to go through such professional training. It's comparable to having a box of tools in your household: The tools come in handy when you need to make small repairs, even if you have no training in the relevant trades. When you have large-scale repairs or renovations, however, you probably hire a specialized firm. Well, this book provides you with just such a DIY toolbox. Experience has shown that giving coaching in small, just-in-time doses can be very effective. Managers can use the tools presented here to develop their staff and increase their own impact.

More impact for managers, thanks to coaching

Leaders are in their natural element when they can drive things, trigger responses in people, set goals and targets, and monitor their achievement. They like to develop strategies and ensure these strategies take effect in their organizations. All these are different forms of impact in a system.

At present, impact in management is impeded by four deficits: 1) ignorance of the systemic conditions, 2) a lack of willingness to acknowledge the facts, 3) unreflected ("knee-jerk") trigger-response patterns, and 4) insufficiently developed people who keep that impact from materializing. In this chapter, I've focused on factors 3 and 4. I have showed you how, as a manager, you always have a choice between two doors – even if you currently face a tremendous overload. Once you have made up your mind to accept the facts of the VUCA world, once you have resolved to work with the people you have, you are ready to adopt a new attitude. You tell yourself: I choose coaching as an additional element of leadership and empowerment. I will develop my staff, so I will have more time for essential strategic tasks. This is how impact begins.

Chapter 1: Takeaways

- Lots of managers feel they lack time for strategic tasks and get too caught up in operational detail. Many have felt that way for years. In the VUCA environment, this situation escalates – so, if you keep on as before, you put yourself and your achievements at risk.
- As a manager (just like everyone else), you always have the choice between two doors. Which one will you walk through: Do you want to keep absorbing more and more responsibility, like a vacuum cleaner sucking up dust? Or do you want to adopt a new attitude and demonstrate true leadership qualities?
- With a new attitude, you may well realize you don't have to do everything on your own. With people who have been appropriately developed, everything gets easier and you have more room to maneuver. You have the choice between recruiting capable people or developing them yourself.
- Developing your existing staff will always be your first choice, as you tend to surround yourself with people you inadvertently attract. To develop people, you need tools. Coaching tools are not your only approach, but one of the most powerful ones.
- You don't need a coaching degree to include a set of highly effective coaching tools in your repertoire of leadership tools. If you manage to trigger positive development in every individual on your staff, you can focus on your essential tasks. With easy-to-learn coaching tools, you will have impact again – at last.

Chapter 2
Engaging your staff through communication – or:
Please use the elevator!

Managers are expected to show empathy, understand their people's needs, maintain rapport with all stakeholders, and ideally provide a strong sense of purpose. Well, isn't that great? No wonder business magazines and guide books are full of fool-proof tips on how to handle demanding employees. Nothing wrong with that, of course. But good intentions can't move mountains. To really engage with your staff through communication, you need a basic understanding of the different personality types and communication styles that exist. You will also need approaches that work. The coaching toolbox offers all of that.

Back home at last, Henk sighed. He had landed at Amsterdam Shiphol at 4:05 p.m., let his Mercedes's driver assistance system guide him through the dense traffic on the A44 to The Hague, and was now looking forward to a relaxed Friday evening. He and his wife Jeanine had plans to meet friends at a waterfront bar later on. He would step into his Wassenaar home only long enough to drop his briefcase. In his 25 years as country manager of an agricultural group, he had welcomed at least as many business partners, functionaries, and politicians at home as he had in his Amersfoort office. The report on his visit to the company's global headquarters in Delaware would have to wait till Monday. Still, he couldn't stop thinking about one thing his young US colleague Carey had said: "You're no longer the king of your cute little dairy empire now, Henk. We are a global player, and you are responsible for all of Europe. It's gonna be a big change for you."

King? Cute? Henk shook his head. It had never bothered him much how Harvard graduates talked about him at headquarters.

In the Netherlands, he had a superb network in place, which was one of the reasons he was virtually irreplaceable. No one could replace him – except for his protégé, the "crown prince," of course, whom he had built up and, after getting approval from Delaware, introduced to his staff as his successor, the new county manager, two weeks earlier. At 60, he felt he was at a perfect age to take on a new challenge. Head of Europe! But change his habits? He didn't think that was necessary. The European headquarters were located between Antwerp and Brussels, just a two hours' drive from home. Also, it seemed to him that managing Europe wouldn't be so different from managing the Dutch operations. His motto was: Know the right people, do them favors every now and then, and rely on your gut feel. So what could be so different?

When he turned on his car's stereo for the 5 o'clock news, Henk realized he had not properly hooked up his smartphone to the console. He touched the "connect" button again and was aghast: Since his plane had landed, the list of missed calls and voicemails had tripled! It was Friday. What on earth was going on? Voicemail No.1: In Italy, people were quitting by the dozens because they thought the Parma plant manager was insane. Voicemail No. 2: The country manager of France ranted on about Carey's suggestion to achieve a 25 percent share of organic products in the next five years, calling it one of her stupid hipster ideas and sounding like Louis de Funès about to throw one of his famous fits. Voicemail No. 3: In Poland, people refused to implement the new gender guideline. There had been an uproar at the workers assembly. Voicemail No. 4: The chief controller of the Denmark operation accused her boss of corruption in his dealings with the EU Commission and threatened to go to the police. Voicemail No. 5: In Greece, production was down again. A decision was needed urgently: he was requested to call back the same day. Henk's face got longer and longer as he went from message to message. "And I'm the one expected to set things straight for everyone," he muttered. His face lit up only when he listened to voicemail No. 6. It was Philip, the young Country Manager in Spain, on whom everyone's hopes were pinned. "Hello there, Henk, hope you're on your way to a nice weekend! Could we speak briefly tomorrow? I have a question."

In the wrong film, all of a sudden …

Henk's situation is not unusual. Many long-serving managers experience the same. They have settled themselves into a certain constellation, their job running almost automatically. Sometimes they have their own hypothesis as to what their success is based on. For instance, they think of themselves as "born leaders." Or they are convinced their gut instincts have never failed them. Or they rely on their network, which is all about giving and taking – including the occasional favor, of course. Hardly ever are they aware that their success is based, above all, on one factor: That they have adapted to the conditions inherent in their system. Any change to these conditions could weaken their impact. And it doesn't matter whether such a change has been brought on by themselves – as in Henk's case – or as a result of sudden external shift. Whatever the case may be, one thing is clear: Unforeseen changes are "situation normal" in the VUCA world. The no-brainer aspects of business – all the routines and established processes – are, or will soon be, a thing of the past. Regional kingdoms are facing turbulent times.

Do I always have to fix things –
or have I failed to engage with my people?

Henk's response to the sudden stress of his new position is to think he can fix everything for everybody. He expects things to run perfectly; when they don't, he makes other people's problems his own. We have talked about typical stress patterns and reflexive responses to them in the first chapter. This chapter will introduce a personality model I find helpful.

Let's begin with Henk: He is a personality type that is quite common in top management – and the same is true for the real-life person after whom I modeled him. To get rid of stress and solve problems, a person of this type does not start by changing his or her own attitude. A person with a strong Thinker element in his personality, combined with Persister elements (see box), has a take-charge mindset, along with good analytical capabilities, and is guided by strong convictions. This person expects his or her people to show strong commitment and independent thinking. People that can't follow intellectually or do not appear committed enough drive this personality type up the wall.

> **PCM: A model to engage your people**
>
> The Process Communication Model® (PCM) was developed in the 1970s by the US psychologist Dr. Taibi Kahler (whom some readers may know as a key co-founder of Transactional Analysis). Kahler had observed that interpersonal relationships tend to follow certain patterns. Depending on these patterns, communication will succeed or fail. PCM allows you to make a rough evaluation of any discussion partner within just a few minutes, based on his or her behavior. This makes the person's behavior and typical stress responses easier to predict. Between 1978 and 1996, NASA used the model – among other things - in selecting astronauts for their missions. Taibi Kahler was a communication consultant to President Clinton in the 1990s, and in this function had quite an influence on the president's speeches and campaigns. Today, the Process Communication Model is applied in coaching, management, people development, and education worldwide.
>
> Contrary to static personality models, the PCM approach does not pigeon-hole people. Every individual has elements of each of the six personality types distinguished and addressed by the

model and listed below. Think of these personality elements as the floors of a building. On the first floor of our personality, we have moved around effortlessly since early childhood. The higher up the other floors are, the less access we have to the elements of the respective personality types at any given point in time, and the more energy we need to muster to "go up" to that floor. This is why we often find it difficult to communicate with people who have easier access to personality elements that differ from our own.

Basically, we have access to all floors. Managers can therefore use the model to learn how to communicate successfully with people of any personality type. It does require some re-learning: We are normally used to concentrating on message content. For successful communication, however, it is much more important to engage with the other person appropriately – that is, in a manner that matches their personality type.

When you are not in touch with other people you can't convey your message either.

The model distinguishes six personality types. One of them is the base type for every individual. In addition, a second type can be strong, too, perhaps even a third. The weakest element is your dormant potential.

- **Thinker:** responsible, rational, and well-organized.
- **Persister:** committed, conscientious, and guided by strong values.
- **Promoter:** convincing, charming, and persevering.
- **Harmonizer:** empathetic, warm, and relationship-focused.
- **Imaginer:** quiet, pensive, and imaginative.
- **Rebel:** spontaneous, creative, and looking for a good time.

Studies have shown that top managers often have a Thinker-Persister combination as their base type. As always, exceptions prove the rule – I have actually met all base types in top management. If you have strong Thinker-Persister elements, your natural communication style is unlikely to engage Harmonizer or Imaginer base types. To communicate as effectively as possible, you'll need to get on the elevator and go up

> to the Harmonizer and/or Imaginer "floors" of your personality "house." Incidentally, the model can also help you recognize individuals' typical stress responses and respond appropriately. As such, the model is a very useful tool for both people development and effective day-to-day communication.

For Henk, everything is about his own values and goals – not those of others. In stress situations, his motto could be: "My way or the highway." In today's work environment with its flat hierarchies, cross-functional collaboration, or even rotating leadership, managers like 60-year-old Henk are bound to feel out of place. In the event of a crisis, they have two options: Either they find their way out of stress – or conflicts will get worse and stress will build up further. In situations like these, coaching can help people with this personality type realize that those around them are not too stupid to solve problems, nor are they insufficiently committed – rather, it is their own communication that fails to engage and empower people. When employees keep receiving signals that tell them their boss is much better at solving problems than they are, they will tend to let the boss go ahead and do it alone. Managers who've understood this have a chance to reflect more and change their communication behavior.

If your "high horse" loses its bearings, dismount and continue on foot

Bursting with self-confidence, Henk leaped at the new challenge as Head of European Operations at the agricultural company. Now he realizes that, just because you play the guitar, doesn't mean you're qualified to direct an orchestra. In his world, everything used to be simple and clear. Everyone knew everyone, and the motto was "Live and let live." His regional organization has kept a distance from the US headquarters, emphasizing its idiosyncrasies. Now Henk is expected to act as a link between headquarters and more than ten country organizations. He is expected to make sure corporate targets are met. And he realizes he is facing a host of regional kings – all of them just as stubborn as he used to be. The French and Spaniards refuse to keep increasing output and lower prices, pointing to their manufacturing traditions. The Scandinavian controller seems to apply stricter ethical standards than her shrewd Dutch colleague. The Italian and Greek managers tend to act out conflicts much more emotionally than their peers. All in all, the country operations each have corporate cultures at different stages of maturity, different degrees of digitalization, and very heterogeneous employee educational levels. Is Henk really ready to embrace these differences?

For Henk, using coaching tools isn't something that comes naturally. The real-life person behind this character first came across some coaching tools when he attended a "leadership journey" program at his company. At this point, that manager thought he already knew what coaching was all about, and that it would not help him. His opinion was set. A typical Persister strength, by the way, these clear-cut opinions. "But I talk to people 24/7 already. How much good can it do to talk even more?" is how Henk would probably put it. It might take him a while to understand the difference between his approach to discussions – communicating his beliefs and principles, making decisions, giving directions, preparing deals – and the kind of conversations used in coaching, which aim to enable people to access their own resources. Let's assume, for the purposes of this story, that a happy coincidence takes Henk to the office of a coach, located at the Keizersgracht in Amsterdam. Let's call that coach Anna. In a series of coaching sessions with her, Henk learns to accept that his people are different from him. He realizes how pointless it would be to try to manage the company's European operations the same way he managed his old "kingdom." He understands that he won't be able to engage people with his usual communication style. But, step by step, he also learns he can get into the elevator to pick up different base types at their respective floors. After several coaching sessions, he faces the upcoming weeks with good intentions: He is determined to get better at engaging his people.

Know your seducers

"One more question," Philip added when Henk was just about to end the call. They had been talking for almost half an hour, another spontaneous phone call. Meanwhile, two visitors had arrived that Hank had kept waiting. Oh well, he thought, she's a journalist; she's probably used to waiting. Still, he wanted to tell her in person rather than delegate it to his assistant. Henk had always been known for good manners. Right now, however, he was eager to implement some learnings from his coaching sessions and work on strengthening the rapport he had with his people.

"Shoot," he told Philip.

"Well, I've got this draft agreement here for our new shipping contractor. I don't know how you handle those things in Holland, but some of the points I am reading here are Greek to me. No pun intended …"

At 28, Philip was one of the company's most promising candidates. He had been made Country Manager of Spain to earn his spurs, so he would be ready to take over when Henk retired and move to the US at some point. That, at least, was what headquarters had planned, and for once it was a plan coming from Delaware that had Henk's full support.

Henk liked Philip. What's more, over the past weeks, he had become a fatherly friend to the younger man. He had traveled to Spain several times, carrying on long conversations with his younger colleague during their joint walks in the countryside. Philip admired Henk, and Henk, for the first time, felt that his knowledge, experience, and past achievements were appropriately acknowledged. Between his visits, he regularly took calls from Philip asking for his advice. They would usually talk for half an hour at least, often longer.

"Listen, the best thing for you to do here …," Henk began after Philip had read most of the draft to him. After Henk had virtually dictated everything Philip was to put into the contract, they had talked for over an hour.

When Henk was finally ready to greet the journalist, she had left a while ago. Her empty coffee cup was sitting on a side table.

Henk's assistant had that "Oh dear!" look in her eyes. "From what I overheard, it seems she was tipped off by someone in Denmark and started looking into the corruption issue," she said. "Now she's going to write that you denied her an interview. At least that's what she told me when she left."

At that point, Henk realized that while he had just solved one problem, he had created another. If Anna, his coach, had been there she would have probably raised her eye brows and asked, "How do you know you've just solved that problem? Because Philip can't make any decisions without you and keeps you from doing your work?"

Why the hand mirror is one of the most important management tools

When managers believe they always have to tell their people what to do, that in itself is a stress pattern. Some believe they can save time by giving quick instructions rather than discussing things at length. But even if that effect occurs temporarily, it is quickly canceled out by the fact that people keep coming back for advice at ever-shorter intervals. There are coaching techniques that managers can use to help their people find and implement solutions on their own. But beware: Coaching techniques are not mobile apps that you can simply download and install. They require a change in your own personal attitude. You need an attitude that enables you to get from "telling" to "asking." Without it, people development will be difficult, and you will wear yourself out.

Every manager with a solid track record of success is highly self-reflective. This characteristic is also essential if you want to use coaching tools effectively: They provide the basis for switching to the meta-level and analyzing other people's behavioral patterns. So, even if you plan to use only the individual coaching tools in your management practice, you will need a minimum of self-reflection. The Process Communication Model® (PCM) helps you – among many other things – to self-reflect and go to a meta-level. The key is to be willing to look in the mirror, reflect, and learn. That is why the hand mirror is one of the most important management tools.

Unmet needs or stress – which is the bigger trap?

An experienced coach like Anna knows how to hold up a mirror for Henk to see his own reflection. She helps Henk recognize his own patterns, in particular his stress patterns, and to understand that in his relationship with Philip, many of his actions cause stagnation and increase the problems on both sides. Unwittingly, Philip and Henk have lured each other into a trap.

Managers are used to getting little in the way of thanks for their work. This is not so tragic for the Thinker-Persister type, as these people get most of their motivation out of their own work. So long as everything runs according to plan, on time, and up to standard, they are happy. But getting recognition for their achievements is often a major unmet need – and very seductive. Why else would managers beam happily when they receive some irrelevant business award from the hands of a politician?

Philip admires Henk for his knowledge and experience. He regularly draws on both. Henk feels flattered and provides plenty of input. As a result, Philip's development is slowed down, and, in the long run, he will be unable to solve his problems, because solutions usually come from his mentor. As Henk faces these same problems with other people as well, he is permanently under stress. As a Thinker-Perceiver, his stress pattern makes him become even more of a perfectionist, explaining much too much, going into too much detail, and delegating much too little. He even dictates the words of a contract to his mentee, just so the problem will go away.

Will Henk and Philip ever get out of this trap? It's a good thing this is not a TV series, so you don't have to wait for the next episode. All you need to do is read on …

Use your elevator

"So you know the ropes now," Henk said, raising his aperitif to toast with Philip. "This will be our last meeting for a while."

"No problem," Philip replied with a grin. "I've got this covered. There's only one last question regarding your handicap. I'll call you about it tomorrow."

Both men laughed. They were sitting on the terrace of the restaurant "El Ganador" in Marbella, right next to one of the local golf clubs, and waiting for the first course to be served. The place was crowded, people around them were chatting and laughing. It was a perfect summer night.

"So, what's new in Parma?" Philip asked.

"Oh, you know, those guys are always looking for trouble. I don't take them that seriously any more. Let them blow off some steam. In the end, they'll get their act together somehow. If they don't, I'll give them a call. I know now how to rope them in again when they get out of hand."

"What about Denmark?"

"You know what? Turns out compliance wasn't the controller's main concern. She had a thing going with her boss. Complicated story. I made sure they sorted things out between them. Now she's dropped all her corruption allegations."

"Greece?"

"Those guys just want some fun at work, or else they'll turn off the machines and pretend they're down. I've sent a real fun guy there as production manager – feel-good manager is more like it – now things are running smoothly."

"How about that French guy?"

"From the Garonne? I decided I let him do his thing. Once you give that guy some peace and quiet, he'll come up with pretty good ideas and solutions. "

"Well, I've learned quite a few interesting things tonight."

"Glad to hear it. But as my successor, you'll do things your way. It's fantastic to have such great talent in our firm."

This last sentence made the elderly lady at the next table look up from her tapas plate and briefly glance in their direction. Henk – radiating charm and ready to network – gave her a friendly "Buenas noches!" slightly raising his glass.

"Guten Abend," the woman replied, continuing in German and introducing herself as Christel Lange. "Sorry for listening in. I heard you speak German, which is unusual because around this time of the year Marbella is full of English people …" She had been coming here every spring, she told them, for more than 25 years. This was her fourth trip alone since her husband had passed away and left her the family-owned business, a lamps and lighting manufacturer. "As a matter of fact, I noticed the two of you the other day on the golf course. It seems you're enjoying your stay here!"

"We are celebrating," Henk let her know, "because this young man here has recently stepped into my shoes, and he's doing very well!"

"That's lovely!" With her plain linen jacket and designer scarf with a Paris label, Christel looked all business and understatement. "You know, our company was established four generations ago. When my husband was still alive, nothing could be changed. He was strictly against it. Now it's time for renewal. We are still doing very well, but we need young people with fresh ideas."

"Why don't you give me some more details about your company," Henk said. Several names had instantly popped up in his mind. "My colleague Ollie, erm, Oliver in Amsterdam is about to leave the company, and he's looking for a new challenge …"

So, a happy ending for Henk and Philip. Let's see what Henk has learned. And Philip, of course. First off, Henk knows now how to escape the typical stress patterns of managers with strong Thinker and Persister elements. There are even moments when he manages to leave the operational details aside. He takes time-outs for reflection and self-reflection, and for the casual exchange with his staff and partners. While he did cultivate ships before, he tended to view people as human resources that had to be selected, deployed, and coordinated in order get something out of them. Before each talk, he would think about what he wanted to get out of it. Now he is capable of going to dinner with his people and show some interest in them and their world. As before, Henk is conscientious, convincing, committed, and highly efficient with his time. But unlike the "old" Henk, he now recognizes the signs when he starts feeling stressed, and shifts down a gear. As a result, his stress patterns no longer lead him to behave destructively. When tempted to preach, give instructions, or criticize sharply, he mentally takes a step back. And while he still likes to pass on some of his vast experience, he leaves it to others to draw their conclusions. Philip, on the other hand, has learned that it is okay to see Henk as a role model, provided that he manages to find his own solutions and take responsibility for their implementation.

The challenge to accept people as they are

Perhaps the greatest learning step Henk has taken is that he is now able to accept the differences between people and to address each person in a way that is appropriate for that individual's particular personality type. To achieve this, he's had to learn how to listen better. Today, he no longer looks at conversations as an exchange of facts. He also listens to nuances now. These nuances – choice of words, tone of voice, gestures, facial expressions, posture – give him valuable clues as to what personality "floor" the other person is currently at and what the corresponding needs are. If these floors are far away from his own current position, he gets into the elevator to go up there. Before, Henk wouldn't have thought he could be expected to care about, let alone meet, his people's emotional needs. He had no time for that. Now he knows that one of those ominous "needs" may simply be the desire to be addressed in the language appropriate for that personality type. While Henk used to spend ten minutes speaking Thinker language to a Harmonizer, he will now say something like "Great you're a part of the team now. We are all there for each other, you can rely on us."

I am aware that some Thinkers may have their doubts about that – but acknowledging a person can really give wings to a Harmonizer type, both personally and in terms of performance.

Stronger impact through more reflection

Studying coaching techniques and using them in day-to-day business encounters can help you enhance your self-reflectiveness and gain a better understanding of the communication and behavioral patterns used by the people around you. Both will immediately increase your impact. Self-reflection enables you to recognize what gives you energy, and how you can be productive using your personality elements. Once you have the energy, your mental needs are met, and you can be successful in ways corresponding to your personality. You'll also need energy for your elevator – the one that will get you up to other people's personality "floors" to pick them up from there.

Among the personality types, there is no "better" or "worse." In management, as everywhere else, we find all of them. Once you know your people's mental/emotional structures, you can predict their stress responses and step in as needed. By addressing each type's mental/emotional needs, you get your people into the boat. That, in turn, makes (senior) staff support you and take some of your workload off your shoulders. There is a broad range of personality models. Familiarize yourself with at least one of them well enough to get to a meta-level (a bird's eye perspective, as it were) that allows you to better understand yourself and others.

Chapter 2: Takeaways

- Too few managers realize how much their impact depends on their being "used to" the conditions in a given system. When these conditions change (or the managers change into different roles), their impact is at risk.
- If you want to use coaching tools in people management, you need to work on your attitude. You need some degree of self-reflection and a meta-level to be able to read other people's communication styles and behaviors.
- Under stress, managers often lose their ability to communicate effectively. Typical stress patterns make it even more difficult than usual to address employees with different personality structures in appropriate ways.
- The Process Communication Model® (PCM) helps assess people's personality elements quickly, to recognize their preferences and strengths, and to predict their stress patterns. This makes the PCM a highly useful tool in people development.

- Once you have studied different personality types and understand their needs and stress responses, you can "use the elevator" to access the parts of your own personality that are usually less accessible to you but better aligned with the other person's personality type in order to "pick up" others with your communication and increase your impact.

Chapter 3
How to increase value contributions – or:
The blessings of coaching

Coaching is one of several ways to develop people. To make the best use of coaching, it is important to leave aside roles and goals and focus on the individuals in those roles. Many managers are a bit taken aback when they hear that. They would like so much more to have capable people fall into their laps, so to speak. Many do at least understand that it's a good thing to develop your staff. The reason is obvious: The more developed people are, the more value they can contribute to an organization. If people are enabled, through coaching, to develop further, they will live up to their capabilities better and more authentically, and serve the organization better – which is what should always be a manager's key concern.

"So, how are things?" At last, Christian had made up his mind and sat down in a chair next to Ralf. He had spotted a free seat at his table. The champagne he'd had at the beginning of the Christmas party, together with the rich, deep-red Cabernet Sauvignon from California's Napa Valley which had been served afterwards, made it a little easier for him to start a conversation with one of the "gearheads" – a term some of the executives used for the company's mechatronics engineers, despite the substantial development the profession had made over recent years. Still, it was quite an effort for Christian – the expat general manager rotated to Charlotte from of one of Lower Austria's largest automotive components suppliers and repair centers – to address Bob, of all people. Bob had been with the company 26 years, and was considered a loser by top management. He always needed an extra push. Christian was certain that Bob simply wasn't as smart as the young guys who had gotten one of the company's coveted traineeships. Well, at least the man was loyal and, after so many years at the company, knew every screwdriver by first name. He even seemed quite popular among the youngsters, something Christian couldn't understand. And Martina, Christian's colleague on the management team, praised Bob for his "social skills."

"Can't complain," Bob muttered, and fell silent again. What a bore! Christian watched Martina talking animatedly with her assistant, and he wanted to join them. In conversations with those two, they would all feed each other the lines and one joke would follow the next. But as a result of his last coaching session, Christian had decided to dedicate more time to his people. Which included Bob. Christian wanted to get better at seeing the personal side in his people. Not to cozy up to them, but to better recognize people development opportunities. "In a constantly changing world," he had told his coach, "we need as much information about people as we can get. Only then will we see potential we can develop." To that, the coach had added, "Successful companies have learned from first-hand experience that, when managers look for capabilities instead of degrees, it is much easier to fill open positions with internal people." Well, this was not really coaching by the book – but the man was right.

As a matter of fact, there was a vacant position in the company that they had so far been unable to fill. Christian and Martina were desperately looking for a new workshop manager in their Charlotte, NC, operation. Bob seemed to be the last person qualified for it, despite his long tenure. A workshop manager had to be able to prepare quotes, assign tasks, take responsibility for the final inspection, write invoices, and, in the event of a dispute with a customer, negotiate a fair solution. No way was that a job for Bob, Christian thought. So they had kept looking around. But the talent market was tight; top people went to the big-name US or European companies and didn't see their dream job in an industrial park south of Charlotte near the long-disputed stretch of the North/South Carolina state line.

"And how's the hobby?" Christian asked, still trying to get a conversation going with Bob. He took another sip of wine.

"You mean, on the Memorial?"

"Sure." Christian had no clue what Bob was talking about. He had no idea what "gearheads" went in for as hobbies. "Memorial" was the name of the Spartanburg airport. Was Bob a pilot? That would be a pretty expensive hobby.

"Well, I've just ordered a brand new HK 36 Super Dimona." All of a sudden, Bob was animated: "We're talking six figures here – so you really need to know your numbers are 100 percent correct and scratch any extras you don't really need. Are you familiar with gliding? No? The Super Dimona is a light, one-engine prop plane. In our soaring club, we use it to pull the gliders up into the air."

"And you're responsible for buying it?" Christian asked, eyebrows raised.

"Yeah, that's my job. I'm the treasurer. I take care of finance and organization. Actually, I'm also in charge of hiring instructors and coordinating classes. Been doing that for years now, it's not such a big deal."

"Tina, could you please come over here?" Christian called across the festively decorated room. His head was spinning.

Hidden champions

Do you know what your people's hobbies are? Do you know what energizes your people, what makes their eyes light up when they talk about it? If you do, you're probably aware of some of your people's hidden potential. Just like all the other stories in this book, the one about Christian and Bob is true. I just put it in a different industry and location and changed the names.

So, here we have a boss that has never really made an effort to get to know his employee, but mercilessly pigeon-holed him as a loser. And while the boss is frantically looking for the right candidate for a position with budget responsibility, he learns one day by chance – in a conversation he only started after having had a coaching session – that the supposed loser happens to be the treasurer of a soaring club. In that function, he's in charge of purchasing decisions in the order of several hundred thousand euro. After this revelation, the boss offers him the vacant position. The man accepts it and proves his worth. He hadn't actually been a loser – he had simply been bored in his old job. More specifically, he hadn't seen a way to develop further and tap into his hidden potential. Only at his soaring club had he found that opportunity. Which is not very surprising, as people there knew him better.

The art of seeing the whole person

Christian worked up the courage to start a conversation with a supposed loser. He did several things that were right. For people of my profession it is easy to say: Starting tomorrow, please pay more attention to the people in professional roles. Very well, a coachee may say, but how, if I've never done this before? Christian takes it one step at a time, and thus improves the odds that his people will open up to him. No one would ever think it was contemplating the sorrow of the world that gave you, the boss, the urge to fraternize on all fronts. "All men will become brothers" is a tune rarely played in companies. Another glass of wine, and it could have gotten dangerous for Christian. But he kept a grip on himself. He didn't come straight to the point, nor did he try to flatter Bob – rather, he expressed an interest by asking questions. The questions did not invade Bob's privacy, but they provided opportunities to have a good talk. Ralf could take them or decline.

Without an atmosphere of trust, it is almost impossible have a good personal talk. Working with his coach and reflecting on what had been said, Christian had realized that the Christmas party would be a good occasion. There may be managers who mistake office parties for drinking sprees, have a few glasses too many, and then watch the situation deteriorate. As a responsible manager you know that "partying" is something you do in your leisure time with your friends. When you participate in company events, while you may not actually be "at work," you are at that event in a specific work-related role. After all, the reason you're invited to company parties is probably because you work there, and not because of your talent for climbing on the table and belting out the good old songs from your youth. So long as everything remains in balance, a casual exchange is possible. Christian approaches the conversation with the right attitude: He wants to learn more about the person – but he is not out to learn something specific. He lets the other man decide what he wants to talk about. He is ready to listen and be surprised.

Identify long-term potential and deliver it in time

Every company has potential that has not been identified, let alone exploited. The reason is that companies are composed of people, and people only live out a part of their full potential. In the previous chapter, you read about the Process Communication Model® (PCM), which helps us realize that certain facets of our personality are easier to access than others. As we are in continuous communication with those around us, it is very important to know what personality elements we want (or don't want) to address in others. The best managers will always be aware of several points to address, even when they don't need them at that particular moment.

Informal talks often provide valuable clues for that. Some managers use their electronic address directory to keep notes on what they know about each of their contacts. This helps them select good topics for small talk. It also helps them collect helpful clues on specific potential that might come in handy someday. If Christian had known earlier that Ralf was a treasurer at a soaring club, he would have probably realized that this "gearhead" had no problem handling quotes and invoices. This kind of knowledge about people's potential increases Christian's impact. He can fill the vacant position at last – with someone that knows the company like the back of his hand. As workshop manager, Ralf can contribute much more value now than before. His old position can be filled with one of the clever apprentices that landed a permanent job at the company. Sounds like a perfect solution, doesn't it?

When the fog clears

For the first time since graduation, Max lit a cigarette. It tasted awful. The 26-year-old assistant to the sales director of a leading insurance company was standing on the small balcony of the brand-new apartment he had just moved into, gazing down at the lights of the Hamburg harbor under a night sky. He was still feeling queasy and hadn't been able to eat anything since his lunch break – or, more precisely, since he had witnessed the two sales managers, Dennis and Mehmet, yell at their colleague Raoul in the parking lot. "It was all my fault," Max thought. His boss, the sales director, was about to decide on a new structure for the company's sales regions. Max had wanted to show his colleagues how important the decisions were that he was preparing, and had talked a little too much at the lunch table. So, not only had the company's three best sales people heard about the director's plans – they also knew that Max had been told to crunch the numbers and prepare a proposal for the new regional structure. Dennis and Mehmet had quickly agreed between themselves on what Max should recommend to his boss: Two smaller regions with the most lucrative customers for themselves

– and one larger region with less attractive customers for Raoul. So, lots of miles every day for Raoul. They had suggested meeting with Max in the parking lot, telling him that under no circumstances was their silent agreement to leak through to management or anyone else.

"You keep quiet, understand?" Dennis had said, practically baring his teeth – so close to Raoul's face that he had lost balance and fallen against Mehmet's Porsche. Dennis was into mixed martial arts, and while he didn't drink, even the smallest provocation could set him off – pretty much like his colleagues after a fourth beer. After talking to Raoul, he had turned to Max.

"Max, my friend," he had said in his smoothest salesman's voice, with his left arm resting on Max's shoulder and pounding Max's chest with his right hand so hard that Max would still feel the pain several hours later, "You take care of this with your boss. Got it?"

On his balcony, Max took a long drag from his cigarette and waited a few seconds before exhaling. Then he took out his smartphone and googled "coaching, conflict resolution."

The next day, Max was sitting on a tan sofa in a small room dominated by a large window on the top floor of a building at Gustav Mahler Platz. It was still light outside, and the window offered a view of the summer sky, iridescent blue and gray. His coach came in: A woman in her mid-thirties, dressed in stylish jeans and an elegant top. "Hi, I'm Susan. What can I do for you?" She shook his hand and sat down in one of the two Wassily chairs across from the sofa.

Susanne seemed just as youthful, outgoing, and uncomplicated as Max had hoped after having had a good look at her website. He also liked the fact that she wasted no time on the first-or-last-name question. Max described his dilemma. He didn't know what to do so that both his boss and the three salesmen would be satisfied. He was afraid of his athletic colleague with his well-toned body, who obviously spent his free time fighting other men based on some arcane or exotic rules. At the same time, he knew his company couldn't afford to lose any of its three best salesmen. He also hated himself for allowing these people to draw him into this power game, just to appear cool to them. He wanted a win-win solution. But how could he achieve it?

Susanne asked him a simple question.

"You mean," Max replied, "Who will make the ultimate decision and take the responsibility? Well, the management board, of course. Not me. I'm just supposed to make a suggestion." He paused a moment. "So what you are saying is … yes, of course. I'll tell Dennis and Mehmet what my role is and that I can't influence the board's decision. That my career depends on my making good recommendations. I am the wrong person for them. If they want something from my boss, they should talk to him. Phew. Don't know whether I'll be able to tell them straight out …"

Six weeks later, Susanne received a long e-mail form Max, telling her how everything had ended. The board had considered Max's proposal – and made a completely different decision. The solution was a big surprise to the three sales managers. But it was sophisticated – and fair. In the end, they all took it rather well.

Shortly afterwards, Max accidently ran into Dennis in the parking lot. Dennis walked toward him, punched him on the shoulder, and said, "Hey man – I knew we were friends."

When the noose tightens around your neck

"Brain fog" – that is often the biggest problem in a conflict situation. Coaching techniques can help clear the fog in someone's head. Often, the fog approaches almost unnoticed. You give in to a minor weakness and allow yourself to be coaxed into risky behavior, which then gains momentum. Or you take a blow that isn't so dramatic but triggers self-doubt that builds up more and more. Max, the young over-achiever and top-management assistant, is a rising star in his company. His boss values his intellectual capabilities, but Max lacks experience. He feels insecure at times because, while he has moved up and into the tower of power, he doesn't want to be bothered with "power people vibes." In the Process Communication Model® (PCM), he is both a Thinker and a Harmonizer. He wants to be everybody's darling and achieve win-win situations every time.

Like many other people, Max gets into exactly the situation he dreads the most. He is caught in a vile power game. He dreads spending time with the salesmen and their somewhat rough manners, and yet he wants to be seen by them as someone with power and influence. He wants respect and a safe position. But what he starts soon gets out of control. At the same time, Max is determined to demonstrate absolute loyalty to his boss. According to Barry Oshry, the systems theorist, Max is in a stress pattern common for people in a sandwich position, the "middle crunch." He is torn between two sides. The result: Brain fog. Max can't see a way out. He forgets what his role is and what it isn't. He has allowed himself to be drawn into a pattern of manipulation and, in the end, he believes he has to follow other people's rules and make their desired solution happen. He feels as if a noose is tightening around his neck.

Rediscover who you are, your capabilities, and your role

It takes just a small coaching question to let Max realize that he has missed an exit on the road to hell. To make a U-turn now, he needs to regain his role and deliver on his potential. His role is to prepare decisions for the board, not make them. He had assumed the wrong role to impress Dennis, Mehmet, and Raoul. He wanted to give them the impression that he was the one who would decide on the new regional structure. All in an attempt to boost his standing with his loud-mouthed, high-testosterone colleagues. Well, that definitely failed. Max needs to go back to the role actually assigned to him. But going back is not enough, if he really wants to resolve the conflict. He now needs to develop further and tap into some of his dormant potential.

Neuroscience uses the metaphor of highways and footpaths running through the human brain. The highways symbolize established behavioral patterns, which we use swiftly and effortlessly. The footpaths are ways that are at our disposal as well. However, as we have only used them hesitantly and cautiously, we find them unfamiliar and difficult to follow. When we take heart and choose one of these pathways, we tap into our hidden potential. Max needs lots of courage to take a new path. He had been bold enough to brag a little when talking to the three sales managers. But then he had to work up the courage to tell them openly that he intended to stick to his assigned role. If Dennis and Mehmet wanted the board to decide in their favor, they would have to talk to the board, not Max. The result: With this genuine self-confidence, he now talked to Dennis and Mehmet as equals. They sensed his inner strength and respected what he said. In the end, Dennis was even willing to believe that Max had suggested to the board what turned out to be a superior solution. In this story, a young man used self-reflection to recognize and tap into his own potential. While he couldn't produce a win-win situation – something only his boss could do – he was able to work towards it and serve the organization's best interests.

Trust me

Sunday afternoon in a small town near Stuttgart, Germany. Following the instructions from his navigation system, Oliver turned into a cul-de-sac in the midst of a deserted industrial district. Here, situated between a Škoda dealer and a beverage minimarket, was where the headquarters of Lange Lamps had to be. So far, all he could see were tall hedges with a parking lot in front. He wondered whether the address was right. Then he saw a tiny little sign: "Lange Visitors Parking." Real low-key, for sure. Oliver parked his rental Audi in the empty lot, took his iPhone out of the cup holder, and got out. Tom, the 31-year-old son of a British banker and a Dutch economics professor, had received a call from Henk, a contact he had made at the Amsterdam Chamber of Commerce, who was currently vacationing in Marbella. What Henk had told him had sounded intriguing. Turn around a German family-owned business? Definitely sounded more challenging than helping yet another hyped start-up secure another load of venture capital. It had taken him less than five minutes to get on the phone and call Christel Lange, the owner. And although his German was poor and Christel spoke English with a thick accent, the two had immediately hit it off. Christel had finally suggested meeting at the firm that upcoming weekend, as she would have just returned from Spain and had no appointments yet.

Walking past the dense hedge, Oliver found a complex of low-rise office buildings in various construction styles dating from the past six decades. An aquarium-like structure with glass doors and square stainless-steel door handles looked like it could be the foyer. A cream-colored Bentley coupé was parked in front, its vanity license plates carrying Christel Lange's initials. Oliver was not interested in cars, didn't even own one. And while he could ramble on for hours about whether Apple had been right in launching the latest iPhone at this particular point, he would have had trouble telling a Bentley from a Porsche. He approached when he heard sounds from inside: Christel was talking on the phone. When she saw him, she got out and gave him a friendly welcome.

"Well, here we are," she said (with a very hard German "r"), leading him through the aquarium-like structure into the building. "Not spectacular, I know," she remarked while both of them climbed the stairs to the second-floor conference room.

"To be honest, I am planning to have this modified, some parts even rebuilt. My husband was always against modernizing it – although we always made good money with this business, which goes back more than four decades. I don't know why, but he never saw the point." They stepped into the conference room. "All that mattered to him was that our products were on display everywhere." She gestured to the gigantic, extremely stylish lamp hanging from the ceiling, which would have been fitting for the foyer of the Guggenheim museum in Bilbao. It was a sharp contrast to the very functional-looking furniture in various shades of brown and tan, which had clearly seen better days.

After they had sat down at the conference table, Christel started talking about the company's history. Twenty minutes later, she had gotten to the 1980s ... Together with Fritz, her husband, she had inherited the business from her father Hans, a grandson of its founder. Soon after that, the Iron Curtain fell, offering them a once-in-a-lifetime opportunity: One by one, they acquired a series of former state-owned businesses in Eastern Europe. Around that time, on one of their golfing trips to Marbella, they also made friends with the agent of a famous designer. From that point on, the Lange success formula was "Designed by Philippe Stork, Paris – Manufactured in Bulgaria." At present, Lange Lamps had active manufacturing sites in 12 former Eastern bloc states. Each country organization was headed by a locally born director, all of them enjoyed substantial liberties. The year before, the company had changed its name to "The Lange Group." It was one of several outcomes of a project with a management consulting firm Christel had hired. The consultants had also urged her to recruit an external candidate to be the CEO. "As the company owner, you tend to think in generations and preserve traditions," the McClancy partner had told her. "A CEO from outside will be an innovator and optimizer, and thus a necessary addition to your company's top team. It will be his task to set the course for maximum performance in day-to-day business."

At the end of that day, Oliver agreed to take the position. Christel took him to a fine restaurant for dinner, and he enjoyed both the five-course menu and the feeling of having done the right thing. From a small fish at an Amsterdam investment firm, he had made it to CEO of an international manufacturing group. His only worry was how to break this to his husband André – especially the fact that his new office was located in a little out-of-the-way town in southern Germany.

One evening seven months later, Anna – the Amsterdam-based coach who helped Henk in Chapter 1 – checked her voicemails after a long working day. One of the messages was from Oliver, his voice sounding desperate. He had zero authority as CEO at the Lange Group, he complained. Christel was a wonderful person, but her two sons – roughnecks and show-offs. But even they were better than those Eastern European country managers he had to deal with every day. A bunch of misogynists, homophobes, and machistas! Couldn't deal with the fact that a woman was at the helm. Trash-talked about Christel behind her back, didn't give a damn about instructions from the head office. What should he do?

Establish personal rapport and build trust

Oliver has substantial experience as an investment expert. As an executive, he has none. Moving from Amsterdam to the German countryside was a cultural shock; then there are those Eastern European country "kings," who've been enjoying nearly total freedom of action for decades. And while Oliver is the epitome of a manager who is good at grasping a situation intellectually and identifying a solution, no one is interested. He would love to tell the Lange people, "Trust me, I know what I'm doing!" – and it's true, he does know. But nobody trusts him, and nobody listens. Together with Anna, he starts drawing up a roadmap.

First of all, he realizes he will have to build rapport. The challenge for him is to be on good terms with people who are on different wavelengths regarding their habits and values. This will take a number of small steps. Next, Oliver learns to change his attitude towards both the owner family and the country managers. Instead of acting the part of the CEO, he should try to be a peer, a fellow manager. By doing this, he will signal to the old hands: I am your new colleague on the management team, I've come to bring in fresh ideas and help everyone create win-win situations. And that's not all. As a last step, Oliver learns to tap into the system's potential.

Magical triad: Leveraging your own, other people's, and the system's potential

The consultants Christel Lange had hired criticized the fact that the country managers each pursued their own purchasing policies, sometimes even buying from the same suppliers at different terms and conditions. Oliver is supposed to rectify that now. Aligning those policies makes sense from an overall system perspective – but the country managers will regard any such action by the CEO as a threat to their autonomy. So, Oliver needs to ask himself: How will I benefit, how will the others benefit, and how will the system benefit? Gradually, he learns to leverage the system's potential. He decides to establish a central procurement function and assign people to it. He gets the country managers' buy-in by convincing them that this will be in their best interest: As they no longer need to dedicate time and energy to lengthy price negotiations, they gain greater leeway to focus on other management tasks. So, rather than forcing them to agree on a consistent approach, he establishes a separate entity as an internal service provider. An elegant solution.

At the same time, Oliver considers what could and should be decentralized from a system perspective. He grants more budget responsibility to the country heads. Also, he gives them more leeway in the HR field: For instance, the option to launch their own succession programs, so they can renew their organizations bottom-up and make them more innovative. His solution, in other words, gives the country managers more decision power – not power for power's sake but in a way that will be good for the overall system. And what's in it for Oliver? He will soon be able to demonstrate that a fresh breeze is sweeping the organization – which means he is delivering on his mission to make the company fit for the future. Last but not least, the company's employees will realize that things are moving, and the company is getting younger, more innovative, and more agile.

Each of the fictional characters in this chapter faced the question of identifying and using untapped potential. It is the most important goal in coaching, and it should also be your goal as a manager when using coaching techniques. Max, the young board assistant, successfully identified his own potential and got himself out of a seemingly hopeless situation. Christian learned to better identify his people's potential by showing a genuine interest in them as individuals. Oliver has done a particularly good job in leveraging systemic potential and finding solutions that will bring benefits for all stakeholders. As we have seen, the greater impact that is achievable through coaching and with coaching techniques can manifest itself at three different levels: The manager him- or herself, peers and employees, and the system.

Chapter 3: Takeaways

- In every organization, there is hidden potential waiting to be tapped to create more value. As a manager, you should focus on three kinds of potential: Your own, that of your staff, and that of the system.
- The best way to identify your people's potential is in personal talks. Make sure you create occasions for these talks, beyond your usual routine ones (such as performance reviews). Ensure that there's a trust-based atmosphere in place, and take it one step at a time.
- In conflicts (and not only there), the greatest problem is often "brain fog." Coaching techniques can help you see clearly and identify possible

ways out. Clarifying roles can be very useful here, in other words, asking: "Who are you in this particular situation?"
- The typical stress pattern in a sandwich position is the "middle crunch" – meaning that someone is torn between those "above" and "below." In a "middle crunch" situation, coaching helps to clarify over and over again what each party can expect and what it can't.
- The art is in leveraging systemic potential and finding solutions that all stakeholders will benefit from. Systemic thinking is a part of coaching. It is about taking a holistic perspective rather than settling for isolated short-term solutions.

Chapter 4
Coaching occasions – or:
Can I actually do something myself?

Coaching can make managers' work easier – even in situations that don't strike you as classic coaching occasions. For instance, they can help you save a creative meeting that has gone haywire, or to masterfully settle a major dispute between staff members. Once you've started helping yourself to the big and colorful coaching toolbox, you will know how to make the right coaching interventions in each situation. This chapter provides an overview of different management situations where coaching techniques are particularly useful.

"By the way, before you leave …," Sarah said to her colleague Lennart at the end of their half-hour conversation. In her late thirties, Sarah was Chief Sales Officer at a pharmaceuticals group in London. She and Lennart were sitting at the long conference table in her office. When she had been appointed CSO a year before, the first thing she had done was throw out her predecessor's old-fashioned desk and monstrous executive chair. Her desk with the computer and telephone system was now seamlessly integrated with the conference table. Her chair's back rest wasn't higher than those of the visitors' chairs. Throughout her one-on-one talk with Lennart, a young over-achiever, Sarah kept control of things in her friendly yet focused and matter-of-fact manner. The mixture of a sharp mind and impressive eloquence reminded Lennart of BBC political correspondents. But now, Sarah's tone seemed different all of a sudden. To Lennart, her "by the way" sounded cool, almost dismissive.

Sarah told him that his participation in the company's high-potential program, for which she had nominated him at his request, had been approved. The program was to start in two weeks. Sarah's assistant would e-mail him further details shortly. After that, Sarah began writing on her iPad. "See you tomorrow."

Lennart felt shaken. Slowly, he rose from his chair. What he really wanted to do was jump and dance with joy. The high-potential program! He was in! But why did Sarah give him the good news like that, in passing, just before the meeting was over? In a tone that sounded like clinking ice? Confused, Lennart trudged out of Sarah's office.

After he had left, Sarah got up to do something she rarely did: She went to the tall windows that bathed her office in bright light, despite the overcast sky, and let her gaze wander over the city – from the cars racing by on the nearby M4 to the airplanes taking off from Heathrow in half-minute intervals. Somewhere back there at the horizon, far into Buckinghamshire, was her old company's headquarters where, almost 15 years ago, she had attended a high-potential program herself. Suddenly all the images and emotions were back. How her former boss had talked her into the program, then lost interest. How she had felt as though she had to struggle for everything. She had learned more than ever before on that program. But her boss had never once asked about her progress. At the end she had resigned – out of deep frustration because she knew she would never be able to apply what she had learned at her company.

She wanted everything to be different for Lennart. Different and better. But how? In just a few weeks, the 9-month development program would be launched with internal and external trainers. A long stretch of time, during which Lennart would frequently be unavailable to her. Well, Sarah thought, that's the way it is. I'll help Lennart, but I'll also make sure I get something out of it. Before he leaves for the program, I'll sit down with him, and we'll decide what his development path should be. The agenda for the program is fine as it is. We'll add our own agenda for him. An agenda that will also be good for me and the company. I'll give him a project on the side to test his newly acquired capabilities. Sarah thought hard ... emerging markets ... Africa ... Nigeria! Africa had proved a hard nut to crack for lots of pharmaceutical players. So, let's see whether Lennart could get them anywhere in Nigeria.

Almost a year later, the top team gathered in the boardroom for a routine meeting. One after another, participants took their seats; the mood was relaxed.

"My God, Sarah," said John, the CEO, who was nearing retirement, "What is it that you've done with our young colleague? He seems like a different person! And he's a hot candidate to head our new emerging-markets strategy. I hope all those development talks you had with that good-looking young man weren't too stressful for you? As my old friend Thomas used to say: Never leave a woman who's at the end of her career alone with a man at the beginning of his."

"Well, we both know how I feel about that kind of talk. It's rather inappropriate, don't you think? But thanks for the feedback on Lennart's development." Sarah had learned long ago how to deal with older men's jokes. And she was quick to counter this one rather drily. She knew that John's shallow cynicism was a cover-up for genuine admiration, and felt deeply sastisfied - - even a bit proud.. As a manager, she had achieved something noteworthy here. And as far as that kind of talk went – she was glad she had found a way to respond which, while making her position very clear, let her appreciate said the core of the message.

Grow, baby, grow

People development: Some managers associate the term not with "give and take" but with "give and continue to give." Middle-aged and older managers, especially, can feel exhausted by the demands of their high-potentials, who like to think of themselves as God's gift to the world and expect to be treated accordingly. Good thing we have development centers and similar programs, so the youngsters are taken care of, and their bosses can have some peace and quiet. That was probably what Sarah's former boss thought when he put the gifted young woman in a high-potential program and never bothered to inquire about her progress. In his defense, I should add that it's not self-evident for a sophisticated program to be complemented by individual development talks and coaching. But it's an approach that offers plenty of potential. To leverage it, you need to regard your employees' development as a long-term plan that is all about giving and taking – and about the additional space you create for yourself as a manager.

Development talk with employees is time well invested

Sarah refuses to let the HR department decide – or leave it to Lennart himself – where his career journey will take him. Instead, she makes a point of investing the occasional half-hour to have a development talk with him. In these talks, the young man defines clear development targets for himself. Rather than springing from the imagination of some HR clerk or trainer, these targets are derived from the department's day-to-day activities. As an especially smart move, Sarah assigned Lennart a real project. That way, he gets genuine feedback from the business on his learning and progress. In other words, he learns a lot and can apply this newfound knowledge right away. He receives valuable feedback not only from the program's evaluators but from his boss, too. This way, Sarah ensures that Lennart's development is sustainable and in the right direction. What's more, she can learn a few things herself. By keeping abreast of what Lennart is learning, and how he is progressing, she brings her own knowledge up to speed. And, who knows? At the end of the day, Lennart might even come up with a good idea on how to actually make money in Africa.

Set the big goal, then take small steps

Developing employees sustainably is the overriding goal. People development is good for the overall system. It ties individuals to the company, so valuable skills and capabilities will remain in the organization. At the same time, managers gain time that they can devote to dealing with strategic issues, as they can delegate more and more tasks to their staff. In addition, coaching can also be used to meet short-term development targets, even spontaneously in seemingly trivial every-day situations. For instance, let's imagine a department head comes to the division manager's office, desperate for advice: "I need help! I've got this rookie in my department who is giving me major problems." In a situation like this, the division manager could help the department head create a basis for mutual understanding with that rookie – by asking a series of coaching questions, such as: "How is this person different from your other direct reports? Is there anyone in the group who gets along with him/her? What does that other person have to say about him/her?" It's always possible the department head suffers from "brain fog," not realizing there's a bridge that might lead to that rookie. And while the division manager probably doesn't know that either, he or she can help find that bridge.

> **Key occasions for using coaching tools**
>
> Managers can use tools and techniques in the coaching toolbox in different situations to trigger certain processes or actions. Here's an overview of key situations:
>
> - **People development:** The showpiece discipline of coaching. People that are neither rookies nor accomplished experts can benefit from the impetus from well-phrased questions. There are three kinds:
>   - **Long-term development.** You agree with your employee on development targets and follow up in regular development talks.

- **Short-term development.** You help the employee find his or her own way to achieve a defined short-term target.
- **Ad-hoc support:** You give your employee the impetus to solve a problem that is blocking him or her.
- **Idea generation:** Coaching techniques stimulate creativity and bring about new solutions.
- **Problem-solving:** Similar to idea generation, coaching techniques help to change perspectives and activate problem-solving energy.
- **Conflict facilitation.** In conflict mediation, you use coaching tools to create the conditions in which the conflicted parties will find a way out.

Sometimes you simply help solve everyday problems that are keeping people from focusing on their work. For instance, a manager once told me how he had needed just a few questions to help one of his employees find the right elementary school for his son. This problem had bothered the young man for quite a while. Another helped an employee identify the right therapy for her chronic back pain. Ad-hoc interventions like these can also serve the long-term goal of helping people develop.

Surprise with an effect

Frustrated, Monika stared at her plate. With a determined stride, she had passed the salad bar in the company cafeteria without so much as a glance at all the fresh organic produce from Austrian farmers, and ordered the sweet main course of the day: A large yeast dumpling with vanilla sauce and poppyseed sprinkles. She had asked for extra sauce. Was she really going to eat this sugary calorie bomb? She knew what her body would do with that kind of food: Instantly add to the fat on her hips. She also knew – and her thoughts started wandering when she smelled the vanilla – what she would probably never achieve in life. A more satisfying relationship, for instance. Or a better job. True, her job wasn't so bad: She was in charge of sales at a regional newspaper with a long-standing tradition in local reporting. Her colleagues were nice people, her boss – the CEO of the publishing house – very charming, her salary above market average, and the food in the cafeteria (unfortunately) excellent. Only one drop of bitterness spoiled the glory: Subscriber numbers were declining. The company just couldn't seem to turn around the sales curve. For several years now, it had been making most of its money with innovative digital business models and offshore investments. Despite all the losses, management would hardly give up on the daily paper – after all, it was the heart and soul of the company and a key link to politics. But as head of sales, she fretted over having to report shrinking subscriber numbers, sales, and revenues year after year. Not one major achievement to speak of.

"Do you mind if I join you?" Alexander, the chief controller was standing at her table, his deep voice snapping her out of her dumpling-centered contemplation. As always, he was wearing an impeccable charcoal suit, his quietly patterned necktie tied in a perfect knot. He waited politely until Monika replied "Sure, have a seat!"

"What are you so worried about, my dear?" Alexander had not failed to notice the expression on Monika's face as she had stared at her meal.

"Oh, you know, same old same old. Another very uncreative creative meeting this morning. Another meeting where we couldn't find answers to the key question: What can we do to stop losing subscribers?"

"I imagine that must be difficult. Us controllers, we sometimes talk about that, too, and we've been wondering whether you've ever asked yourselves the reverse question: What we would need to do to lose even the last subscriber."

"Interesting thought. Perhaps we should."

"So, what would the answer be?"

"Let's see … One way would be to take weeks to answer e-mails. Or not respond at all. Rebuff complaints, be arrogant. Fail to update our address database. Raise prices when competitors have just reduced them. Have a website that's not responsive. Charge the same for a digital subscription as we do for the print one. Create ugly and useless mobile apps …"

"Isn't that just what we've been doing?"

Monika froze. Alexander had a point there. Her face lit up. "You know what?" she told him, "This is great! I mean, your question. I'll make sure at our next meeting we'll discuss this precise question: What would we need to do to lose even the last of our subscribers?"

"Then you'll realize that we are doing 80 percent of these things already."

"Exactly. But I have a feeling this will be a breakthrough. It will help us develop new ideas. All we need is a neutral facilitator, someone to ask us provocative questions like this …"

"Any chance you're talking about me?"

Monika smiled broadly, cut off a large piece of dumpling with her fork and dipped it in the vanilla sauce.

The internal coach – a guarantee for genuine solution energy

With his half-joking remarks, Alexander, the controller, inadvertently asked for the role of internal supporter or mentor – you could almost say "coach" – to loosen the gridlock another department is in. Deeply frustrated by the many setbacks they've had over the years, the sales team has failed to solve a pressing issue and come up with new ideas. Monika, the head of sales, is quick to realize how much creative power Alexander's provocative question could unleash. She would love to have him as a guest facilitator at their next creative meeting.

Odd as it might seem at first, this idea might just strike pay dirt because it combines three systemic success factors:

One – an internal coach is a wonderful solution here: While he is not immediately affected, he feels co-responsible because he works at the same company. For the same reason it will be easier for him to establish trust than it would be for an external facilitator.

Two – coaching tools will be applied in a setting spanning more than one department. This can be particularly helpful in making problem-solving or idea generation sessions more productive. A colleague from another department will be familiar with the company; at the same time, he or she will be able to approach the subject without the departmental bias.

Three – having someone from outside the department ask provocative questions will create a surprise effect for the team. With no one in sales expecting anything like that, everyone will be rattled. Which can help to achieve a change of perspective – a key factor in generating the energy to find a solution.

In the real-life situation on which this little story has been modeled, the intervention with this particular coaching question caused a healthy shock. People realized that they had been doing lots of things they shouldn't be doing. That was the breakthrough. All of a sudden, improvement ideas kept popping up. What's more, these ideas were implemented and measurable improvements were achieved.

Getting from Where to How with coaching tools

According to established theory, the primary purpose of coaching is to give people the impetus – spark the ideas – that help them unleash their potential. The larger purpose is to improve relationships between individuals in social systems in such a way that both the individual and the system will benefit. To achieve that, the coaching toolbox has been getting bigger and bigger over the decades. At some point, someone realized that many of those tools could be used for other purposes as well. Everyone knows these effects from their daily lives. You purchase a high-pressure cleaner for your terrace – then you realize you can use it to clean your bike. (For the purposes of this metaphor, let's leave aside the fact that it won't do your bike any good to remove all the grease on the chain.)

Coaching tools are a great help not only in developing the Why or What, but also in getting from the What to the How – that is, when you need a tangible solution to a problem, or a new idea. Let's assume, for instance, you want to enter the South American market – a situation where you know what you want, but you don't know how to achieve it. If you now address the issue too directly in an idea generation session, there's a major risk of lengthy theoretical discussions or even a deadlock. When that happens, coaching questions can help "air" people's minds and refresh the momentum. "What would we have to do to fail?" is one way of approaching this.

Men at the top

"How much longer?" Peter groaned. The climb had been dragging on for three hours now. The July Alpine sun was beating down on them relentlessly. Sweat was running down his face, his short-sleeved shirt had turned into a wet rag. He would have loved to chuck it off, but then his untrained body would have been exposed to Conrad's and Martina's eyes. A nightmarish thought.

"Thirty more minutes and we'll be at the lake," Martina called back to them. Up in her pole position, she was almost 60 yards ahead.

Conrad, walking in between the two with a bit more distance from Peter than from Martina, quickly glanced back, then up again.

Peter grunted. Even now, he could not see a drop of sweat in the other man's haggard face. Only that look of iron determination. Peter gasped for air. He felt dizzy.

Conrad, on the other hand, silently wondered whether Martina knew what she was doing. But he didn't let on to his doubts. The CFO Europe of a global, Japan-based automotive supplier, he never gave away anything – least of all, doubts or insecurities. Perhaps he should have hired a more professional coach to resolve his conflict with his former colleague Peter, now one of his direct reports?

Initially, everything had seemed so right: He'd known Martina for ages from the chamber of commerce. A co-managing director at one of Lower Austria's largest automotive components suppliers and repair centers, she had recently completed a coaching training in the US with Han H. Hirshberg (no less!). Now she was eager to apply her newfound skills.

When she'd heard about the trouble between Conrad and Peter, she had immediately volunteered a friendly offer: A free coaching session. It made a lot of sense to Conrad. He perceived Martina as empathetic – at least, much more empathetic than he thought himself to be, sober realist that he was. Besides, Martina was familiar with the sometimes harsh ways and factual constraints in the automotive sector.

Martina, all optimism and blessed with the best physical condition of the three, was looking forward to the coaching talk. Bravely, she trod in her guru's footsteps. "Forget about coaching on couches," Hirshberg had urged them. "I take my clients to the most unusual places I can think of." Well, the most unusual place for a coaching sessions that Martina – of average imagination –

had come up with was situated at 5,500 feet in the Tyrolean Alps: It was a small lake she had discovered a few years ago, on a hike with her husband.

And there it finally was! Deep green and smooth as glass, surrounded by rubble and a few mountain pines, the lake lay before them. The silence was almost eerie. When they had reached the shore, Martina swiftly put up a sun sail and laid out three meditation cushions in its shade, so they could sit comfortably on the stony ground. Finally, she produced a large bottle of lukewarm Evian to be shared by everyone. Ready to go.

Martina: "Conrad, what would be a good outcome of this conversation for you?"

Conrad: "I've been telling Peter for months what I need of him, but nothing happens. I tell him to get the restructuring effort on the way. I tell him he will get three extra people for that. How much longer will it take for him to get things going? Perhaps you can tell me whether I'm talking nonsense, or why else he can't seem to understand me?"

Martina: "Peter, what are you hearing?"

Peter: "Conrad thinks I'm incompetent. Although I haven't wasted a dime for over ten years."

Martina: "Conrad, what are you hearing?"

Conrad: "He keeps emphasizing how thrifty he is. But for the restructuring effort, we are facing now, we're going to need to spend some of that money."

Martina: "Conrad, would it be correct to say that Peter was a role model for others when it was important for your firm to economize?"

Conrad: "Yes, that's true. When it comes to cost efficiency, he's our best man."

Martina: "Peter, what are you hearing?"

Peter: "At last! This is the first time I hear him mention something I've done well."

Martina: "At this point, I want the two of you to tell me what you most want each other to do."

Conrad: "I want Peter to step on it and get that restructuring project going."

Martina: "Peter, what do you need from Conrad to do your part successfully?"

Peter: "Well, for starters, it would be great if he could stop picking on my weight. That includes the jokes he cracks behind my back."

When the true conflicts come to the surface

No, you don't need to climb a peak in the Alps to have coaching talks. On the other hand, you may want to take more time than Martina did for this particular conversation (which I've shortened, of course.) But what is your take-away from this scene? What do you think was key to resolving this conflict? And why did Peter start talking about his weight towards the end – didn't that strike you as odd? Conrad and Peter are focused businessmen working in a challenging industry. They are under brutal cost pressure, which they have to pass on to their suppliers. Just-in-time delivery is standard, the highway is their warehouse. In a tough environment like this, managers tend to be driven by time constraints and results pressure. There's little talk, no small talk. It's the perfect environment for Conrad, a man with strong Thinker and Persister elements as outlined in the Process Communication Model® (PCM). His "currencies" in dealing with others are logic and values. He perceives the world based on his intellect and identifies and categorizes both people and things based on facts and his own observations. His people appreciate his logical, responsible, and well-organized management approach. For him, key motivators are the acknowledgment of achievements and structured processes.

Peter, on the other hand – Conrad's former colleague, now his direct report – has a pronounced Harmonizer element. His perception of people and things is primarily driven by emotion. His team has been devoted to him for many years; they value his compassionate, warm-hearted, and sensitive nature. His currency is empathy. For him, key motivators are appreciation and sensory experience.

What both of them have in common, along with many other top managers, is a strong Persister element: They are quick to make sound decisions and make informed opinions. Both are conscientious, committed, and good observers. So why aren't they getting along better? The answer is simple: What we are seeing here is a clash of different personal stylesin stress mode. Peter has been brought up believing that savings are essential, and he finds it hard to loosen up. In addition, at a personal level, being overweight makes him feel uneasy. Every small hint at it is a blow to his ego. To top it off, the company is going through a difficult phase – time and performance pressures are high, and there is little room for personal talks.

So, what we are looking at is two people with vastly different dispositions who hardly talk to each other. Oh dear. Without this joint reflection initiated by Martina, Peter would probably have quit the company. His letter of resignation was ready, stored on his computer. But now, everything has changed. Peter musters the courage to talk about his needs. Conrad, though hesitant at first, is willing to acknowledge them. As a next step, Peter can warm to the notion that this is not the time for savings, and he will need to invest in restructuring instead, even hire extra people. They can move on at last.

Shedding light on the situation to enable self-help

Once again, the disagreement on business issues is a minor point. As happens so often, there is another issue behind it. Both men are all about being right, plus there are some vulnerabilities. Above all, there are things unsaid. The turning point in their conflict actually is the moment Peter finally works up the courage to address his hurt over the jokes about his weight. Conrad, on the other hand, would have never believed Peter's weight could be an issue. He had probably never even joked about it, and wouldn't. Not out of empathy but because the issue didn't seem interesting to him. After all, it was none of his business, was it? His rare remarks about Peter's weight are due to that very fact: It doesn't interest him. Yet the combination of these factors has caused a deadlock.

This is another real-life story, with slight modifications. When you moderate conflicts, you need to be prepared for unexpected causes to come to light – which is why it's essential to be particularly observant when using coaching tools. Even if the conflict seems straightforward at first, make sure you listen actively and empathetically and keep asking patient questions. Don't jump to conclusions. Above all, make sure the parties involved listen to each other.

In this chapter, I have described three very different and complex situations. Sarah's and Lennart's story was placed in a corporate setting where HR was doing quite a lot in terms of people development; the key here was to create a win-win situation. Monika needed impetus – fresh thinking – to solve her problem. She and her team needed a change of perspective, as they hadn't been able to come up with creative ideas. Conrad and Peter were stuck in a conflict that kept them from serving the system they worked in as best they could. What do all these situations have in common? A person helps others to help themselves. This person, who is in a coaching role, unleashes the dormant potential in others, ensures new perspectives, or brings hidden issues to light. According to a common definition, which I also follow in this book, coaching means helping people to help themselves. (More on that in the next chapter.) To provide his kind of help, it's essential to create a respectful setting, listen empathetically, and ask the right questions in the spirit of appreciative inquiry – neither too direct or harsh, nor too gentle or soft for the specific coachee and situation.

Chapter 4: Takeaways

- People development should be give-and-take. So, even when HR seems to be taking care of everything, it can make sense to set specific development targets and have regular development talks.
- Long-term and sustainable people development is the overarching goal in using coaching tools. It benefits the overall system and strengthens people's loyalty to the company. Coaching can also be used to provide ad-hoc help.
- Coaching tools are great when it comes to changing perspectives, generating creative ideas, or solving problems in creative ways. My advice here is to cross departmental borders to identify internal coaches or facilitators.
- When managers help people resolve conflicts among themselves, coaching tools can help identify the true causes. Conflict facilitation enables people to listen to each other and find possible solutions themselves.
- Whatever the particular situation may be – be patient, ask questions, and don't jump to conclusions. It can take some time for people to come up with a solution. Also, be prepared for a solution that may surprise you!

Chapter 5
Helping people help themselves – or: Just ask the right questions

Managers need to adapt their leadership approach to specific situations and, to do so, they can make use of different tools and techniques. Today's leaders need to be mentors, advisors, teachers, on-the-job trainers and, yes, sometimes, coaches. Provided they're willing and they've acquired at least a small repertoire of coaching skills. The art is in realizing what the particular situation calls for. Once you master that, you'll be able to switch between different approaches. Coaching is the right approach wherever asking good questions can help people help themselves.

With its graded ascending seat rows, the auditorium reminded Thomas of a movie theater. Somewhere out there, behind the honey-colored wood-paneled walls, Singapore's marina would be glistening in the sunlight now. Here, in the room at Raffles City, 250 top managers from global corporations were sitting in the dim light, hanging on to every word from the lips of a haggard elderly gentleman in a charcoal suit. He was sitting in one of the stylish armchairs up on the stage, bathed in bright spotlights, and talking like a waterfall, leaving just enough time for the host to throw in a cue every now and then. Martin Kale, the initiator and chairman of the Global Digital Transformation Forum – or GDTF – in Singapore, knew how to play to the galleries. Which didn't make it any easier for Thomas to listen quietly for hours. The CEO of a Swiss-based chemicals company, born in Pittsburgh before Eisenhower's presidency, Thomas was an Old Economy veteran. He had moved to Switzerland 20 years ago, not least due to the quality of life, and was now married to Paulina, wife number three, a Czech model. Thomas had steered the company through the great M&A waves of the late 1990s and early 2000s, managing to maintain its independence, and the

Supervisory Board wouldn't dare think of replacing him. So, he could have been looking forward with confidence to his last years as an executive – if it wasn't for digitalization. Thomas was about as excited about the digital age as if he had been sent back to high school, at his age. But, hey, at least he was here now on the tail-end of a trip to China, at this event called GDTF. Which proved he didn't close his eyes to reality, instead listening to what companies like his were facing in the near future.

... and that is why digitalization will revolutionize every single field of business, Martin Kale was saying. *We'll go through unprecedented change at a global level. The pace of change is enormous, and so are the economies of scale that come with it. Different fields of innovation will be connected in ways we've never seen before. Gigantic data volumes will ...*

Holy shit, thought Thomas as the chairman of the GDTF went on and on. It suddenly dawned on him what digitalization really meant. And where his own company was standing at the moment: At point zero. What could he do?

... smart environments will make today's forms of management largely superfluous. As early as 2025, controlling might be carried out by artificial intelligence. Around the same time, we expect to see the first AI robot to take a seat on the Management Board.

Thoughts were racing in Thomas's mind. Damn. We really need a – what did Kale call it? – a Chief Digital Officer. Yes, a CDO – the sooner the better. I'll call Laura when we break for lunch (Laura being his Frankfurt-based headhunter). But Laura will only tell you, a second voice in his head chimed in, that all the good people are with Google, Apple, or Facebook, and that they won't be willing to leave. Not even for a suitcase full of money. She'll say that, if we're lucky, we'll be able to attract the second- or third-best. Okay, point taken. Then she'll bring me one of those hipster types with horn-rimmed glasses from Berlin or Leipzig. With a brain that works fully digitally and no clue about running a business. That rookie probably won't get along with people, let alone know how to recognize a good deal. Shoot.

... Managers need to be prepared to fundamentally change both their attitudes and their organizational principles. Silo thinking has become obsolete. Everyone needs to learn everything from scratch. As Isaiah Berlin, the philosopher, would put it: In the digital world, it's is better to be the fox than the hedgehog.

Okay, so if I can't have it all, I'll need to set priorities. I want an absolute genius to take care of all that digital crap. I want him at the board table, or at least as Chief Advisor to the Board. I want him to have authority, so he can get things going. He can't take directions from our old IT people. If we have a revolution, as Kale says, I want a true revolutionary. Organizational issues? Human resource management? I'll coach him. Or her. Yes, that's how we'll do it! So, when's the frigging coffee break?

... at the end of the day, it's easily possible we'll see the end of the Anthropocene, the age of humankind. So, the future is uncertain – but we shouldn't let that paralyze us. As Ray Kurzweil once said, "Our expectations about the future are linear, but the realities of information technology are exponential."

Push or pull?

The long-established Swiss chemicals company is facing an interesting constellation. Thomas, the old warhorse and colorful character in management, is determined to start a revolution before retiring. Unfortunately, he has no clue as to what digitalization is all about. Which is why his headhunter is going to introduce him to Daniel, a young genius in everything digital, who doesn't know a thing about the organization structure of a chemicals group. The big difference between the two is, Thomas can live comfortably with his knowledge gap, as long as he brings in people like Daniel and empowers them as needed. Having fended off a number of takeover attempts in the past, he is virtually unassailable. Daniel, on the other hand, is leading a dangerous life. His ignorance of what holds an organization together from the inside might lead to his failure at some point. He needs an experienced mentor to prevent his efforts from being thwarted by employee resistance. Then, there is Bruno, the veteran head of IT, hero of days past. Once upon a time, he had given the company a model IT architecture. Now, everything is on trial. How will Bruno respond to Daniel's efforts to "get things going"?

How coaching differs from monitoring, training, and consulting

Thomas decides to coach Daniel, hoping to prevent foreseeable problems. A CEO coaching a younger CDO – is that feasible? Yes and no. Thomas will certainly have plenty of opportunities to assume the role of coach, but that won't be enough. In view of Daniel's lack of experience with all things organizational, he will also have to be his teacher, mentor, and advisor. In keeping with the concept of agile leadership, it will depend on the particular situation as to which of these roles is appropriate and what approach is helpful.

This is a good point to sort out a few things. What, exactly, is coaching? According to the understanding adhered to in this book, it means helping people to help themselves. Whenever you want to develop someone – no matter what age – or enable that person to solve a given problem, there are two basic options: Push and pull. Push means: I'm going to solve your problem for you. Pull means: I help you realize how you can solve your problem yourself. The latter is coaching – a form of non-directive communication.

Its most directive form is teaching. Teachers know all the answers and tell others what to do. This may sound somewhat intimidating at first, but it's a good thing. Just imagine a skiing instructor trying to coax the basic skills from a beginner, "Think about what other techniques you could use, besides the snow plow, to come to a stop." Accidents would be inevitable. A softer form of directive communication is training. Here, the person trained can bring in more of his or her own ideas, with a stronger focus being on learning by doing. Then, about halfway between push and pull, there is a point where you make suggestions that the other person implements independently. This is where consulting and mentoring are located. The least directive type of communication is coaching. You learn *from* a mentor, but *with* a coach. In other words, the coach is on a par with you, does not have the answers ready, and will hold back his or her opinion. You, the coachee, are the expert who will identify the solution.

> **What coaching is and what it isn't**
>
> Coaching is a non-directive form of communication, as is the use of coaching tools by managers. It is all about pull, not push. When you assume the role of coach, you switch from telling people what to do to asking them questions. By doing this, you help them to help themselves. The person you coach basically has all the answers, but still needs some impetus from you to identify an appropriate solution.
>
> **So, coaching is ...**
>
> - helping people to help themselves.
> - agile, situation-specific, and goal-oriented
> - a dialog of equals
> - supporting people in their development
> - never limited to the task or function, always including personal aspects.
>
> **Coaching is not ...**
>
> - mentoring – as mentoring means to learn from somebody
> - consulting – as consulting is more about advising than asking open ended questions

- training or teaching, as coaching is not about imparting knowledge
- psychotherapy, as the focus is not on life crises.

Using coaching techniques, you enable your people to solve their own problems. You do not solve them for them. At the start of a coaching talk, you usually don't know the solution either.

Agile leadership at its best: Constantly adjusting the slider

Directive and non-directive communication can best be imagined as a flowing continuum between the two poles, push and pull (Figure 4.1). Now imagine you have your hand on a slider, so in your talks with employees you can steplessly adjust the settings between the two extremes. That is how it works in management practice. In a half-hour talk with the same individual, you may move the slider several times, going from teacher to advisor to mentor – and coach. The next chapter will address the prerequisites that a person needs in order to be "coachable" – so you will be able to move the slider all the way to "pull." At this point, it is important for you to understand the basic principle of the slider, and to understand where coaching tools have their place.

Managers often believe they need to have an answer to everything. The more so if their career path has led from a technical to a management position. Technical experts feel at home on the "push" side. That's not a flaw. It's a natural consequence of the experience they've gained in the course of their school and university education, as well as in their previous career. Now when someone used to years of push communication gradually expands his or her repertoire to include more pull, there is always a risk that person will soon backslide into explaining to everyone how everything works. For most managers, the attitude they need to adopt as a coach is new territory. So please, be patient with yourself. It is worthwhile developing your pull communication skills. Especially since you know now that you don't need to give up your other communication styles. On the contrary: Wherever called for, you will continue to impart knowledge or give advice. Once you've read this book to the end, you'll also know when it is most helpful for a person to ask just a few questions, so they can find solutions on their own and develop further.

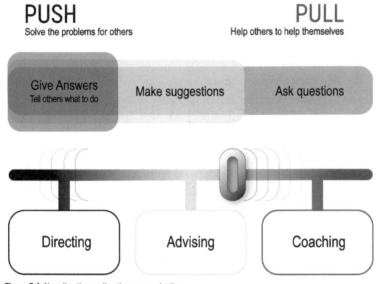

Figure 5.1 Non-directive vs directive communication

Re-imagine!

Daniel was glad he hadn't given up his apartment in Leipzig. For four months now he had been going back and forth. Every Monday morning he would fly to Switzerland – always with a plane full of eastern German construction workers, warehousing specialists, and truckers, who were urgently needed in Switzerland and, by the standards of their home region, paid extremely well. Unlike them, sitting in the back rows, Daniel was no longer interested in money. With a truly ingenuous idea, he had turned his start-up company into a "unicorn," then sold it to a Silicon Valley competitor at a fantastic price. After that, he had spent a year on the Canary Islands with his girlfriend – always true to his motto: Never work again! After a while they had gotten bored, then they had separated, then Daniel had returned to Leipzig. And one day Laura, the headhunter, had called and asked him whether he was interested in a "unique challenge." Would he like to totally dismantle an Old Economy dinosaur, then put it back together and make it into something new? Why not? he thought. He had an appetite for creative destruction.

Now Daniel was sitting at a nicely laid-out table in the Splendour at the Mumbai Orion, with what was, indeed, a splendid view of the ocean and Marine Drive (locally known as the "Queen's necklace" for its twinkling golden streetlights), waiting for Thomas. The people he used to know in his former business life would have texted him to let him know they were ten or twenty minutes late. Not Thomas. It fit his general impression of the company: People seemed old-fashioned, slow, and somewhat strange. He had also heard from a trustworthy source what they for their part thought of him: Snooty, ignorant, not interested in people. Also, they said he spoke a kind of German that no one understood. In short, he was regarded as an alien who did not fit in.

Should he give up? In his world, that was not an option. He was convinced he was doing just the right thing – he had even scouted Chennai for digital back-office support – and he did not expect gratitude. One day, he would leave this company with his head held high, knowing he had made a difference. Achieved something big. The biggest turnaround in the company's history. And more than that: The company's re-invention after 130 years. He also knew that he needed the others' support. If they blocked his plans, he could forget all about disruptive change. So, one way or another, he would have to get them into the boat. But he was determined not to move an inch. Not one inch!

That very second, Thomas came in the door. His presence immediately drew all the waiters' attention to him. Three of them rushed to greet him, respectfully addressing him by his name, and guided him to Daniel's table. On the way there, Thomas cracked a few jokes that made them all laugh. Then he greeted Daniel with a jovial pat on the back and sat down. As always, he showed not the slightest sign of stress or time pressure, instead looking deeply relaxed. He enjoyed their five-course menu as much as their small talk, which ranged from Thomas's views on India's top chemical companies, a few sights in Mumbai, and his excursion years ago in the Himalayan foothills via the Darjeeling Mountain Rail narrow-gauge "toy train" to his rankings of Switzerland's best trains, ski resorts, and vineyards. Daniel, on the other hand, remained quiet and tense throughout their entire dinner. The whole time he waited for Thomas to get down to the nitty-gritty. Would he reproach Daniel for the bad mood in the company, and the meager results he had to show so far? Would he offer some fatherly advice? Or would he wait till after dessert to tell him, in the same cheery mood, that he was fired?

To Daniel's great surprise, Thomas did none of these things. Over an excellent cognac, he only asked him a few questions. What was his most positive surprise at the company? What was his most negative one? What did he consider his most important contribution so far? What share did others have in it?

This went on for quite a while. With each reply, Daniel calmed down a bit more. And became more and more pensive.

Finally, Thomas asked him: "What are the most outrageous kinds of resistance you are facing at the moment? And how are you going to leverage them?"

Thoughts were spinning in Daniel's mind. The espresso he had ordered had long gone cold.

When it's enough to ask the right questions ...

At the chemicals company, no one but Thomas wanted Daniel there. And Thomas only wanted him because he had understood Martin Kale's keynote speech as saying that people with Daniel's mindset embodied the future in the present. And thanks to his experience, Thomas also knew what would happen when an overachiever of digital change with absolutely no knowledge about organizational issues met his people. So, what is he going to do now, seeing as the mood is down, and things aren't moving? Let's begin with what he's *not* going to do because it is really important. Thomas is not going to make any accusations. And why should he? He is facing exactly the situation he had expected. Also, he's not going to share with Daniel any of his knowledge about organization or management, nor will he give him fatherly advice. At least, that won't be a priority, and it won't happen at this decisive meeting.

What Thomas actually thinks is: This younger man, with nothing but his creativity and business skill, managed to build a start-up company that got Silicon Valley's attention. No one had taught him how to do that. With that in mind, I would trust him to be able to help himself, and to find a way to rebuild this company and also engage its people. So, all I'll do is ask a few questions to activate his grey matter. He can do the rest. Consequently, in this conversation Thomas moves the slider all the way from Push to Pull. He opts for coaching, and it doesn't matter whether he would actually call it coaching or whether he does the right thing intuitively because of his innate talent for people leadership. Daniel begins to change his perspective. In addition to what's *not* working, he begins to see what is working already. For the first time, he starts perceiving resistance as an opportunity. And there is something else Thomas triggers: Daniel learns the technique by being exposed to it – which makes him wonder whether perhaps he should ask his people, who are not particularly fond of him, a few questions.

Corporate culture cannot be influenced directly

While our young protagonist is pondering these things, let us consider another aspect. This story is very much about corporate culture. As a typical facilitator of digital change, Daniel wants to launch a profound cultural change. He's planning to totally dismantle the "joint" and rebuild it again. At the end of the day, this change is supposed to be like a "re-invention." For Daniel to have even the slightest chance of success with his plan, he'll have to realize that corporate culture cannot be influenced directly. Corporate culture can be understood as located at the center of a systemic triangle: At its top we have vision, strategy, goals, and programs. On the lower left we have structures, processes, and routines; on the lower right, skills, functions, and resources. These are the three levers Daniel can pull to achieve cultural change. Anything outside the systemic triangle will affect the culture on the inside.

The company's employees think Daniel doesn't fit in their culture. And, indeed, he feels like a stranger, since this corporate culture feels completely outdated to him. Any discussion about that would be pointless, however. Focusing a coaching talk on the question, "What are we going to do with our culture?" would not make any sense. Thomas is probably aware of this. He knows a management team can influence the culture, but not directly. Cultural change is a process spanning several years. The question is what levers to pull. Will they need a new strategy? Are processes outdated, should they get rid of the silos or hierarchy levels? Should employees go through a development program? Do they need new people with different skills? Most experienced managers would know what levers to pull. But let's suppose Thomas wants to share this knowledge with Daniel. Will coaching questions be enough? Probably not. In a case like that, Thomas would have to move the slider just a little towards Push and give Daniel some insights and well-chosen advice.

Kickoff

They were stuck in a traffic jam. "Mer chan nüüt ändere," muttered the Swiss Uber driver, which his passenger understood to mean there was nothing he could do. Daniel was just about to send Bruno a WhatsApp message to tell him he would be ten minutes late, when he realized Bruno was not on WhatsApp. What should he do – send his IT manager an SMS? Stone Age communication – really? He hesitated. Then he pulled himself together. He wanted to change, after all. He wanted to accept people as they were and make more of an effort to connect with them. He had made some progress already – for instance, by getting Bruno to meet him for an after-work beer in his favorite bar. Just like that. It was a soccer bar. To Daniel's surprise, the driver knew the address by heart. Tonight, FC Basel would play an away game against Foulster United. A European League match. Daniel was not really interested in soccer, but there was a major advantage to this: They wouldn't have to talk all the time. Should the communication turn out to be a disaster, they could simply watch the game. It was just over an hour until kickoff.

With a determined stride, David entered the bar and immediately signaled to a waiter. Did he know Bruno? he asked, and was he already there? Instantly all eyes were on him. (A few weeks later Bruno would tell him why: No one had ever entered that bar with such an arrogant attitude.) The waiter pointed to a niche. David walked over and sat down with Bruno, who was friendly enough but seemed somewhat nervous and tense. Was that because of the game, which was supposed to be the most important of the preliminaries? Or was it his own fault?

After he had ordered a beer, Daniel began asking Bruno a series of questions. Have you always been a soccer fan? What do you like about this bar? What was the best game you ever saw? Can you explain the Swiss Super League to me? With each new question, Bruno's reply was a bit longer. At some point, he was in his element.

Two nights before, Daniel had dreamed about Bruno. In his dream, Bruno had been alone in a windowless basement, at the end of a long hallway. Dressed in a white lab coat, he was sitting in front of a row of old-fashioned computers. The scene reminded Daniel of pictures of the control room at the Chernobyl nuclear power plant. With a manic gaze in his eyes, Bruno was staring at the screens, one by one. He seemed to be in his own world. Daniel pushed aside that memory and paid attention to what Bruno was saying. He listened carefully, threw in an occasional remark, and asked about details from time to time.

After about an hour, Daniel's questions started moving towards work. "Hey Bruno, why don't you tell me a little about the times when you came up with the current IT architecture. What was that like? Was there any resistance? And how did you deal with it?

As it turned out, not very long ago, it had been Bruno who was the bogeyman. His vision of integrated data storage based on the latest software had met with plenty of opposition, as people were fond of their isolated solutions. Animatedly, he told Daniel the story of how he had fought this battle and won. In the process, it seemed as though he was starting to see Daniel with different eyes. Then the game started. Everyone fell silent, all eyes were on the screen.

"I really enjoy talking with you," Bruno suddenly said, after the referee had blown his whistle.

Later that night, when Daniel stood in front of the bar, pulling out his iPhone and opening the Uber app, he remembered Bruno's remark. He smiled. Talking *with* him? Daniel hadn't said much. He had listened and asked questions. But Bruno was a really nice guy. It was a pity that HR would offer him an early-retirement package pretty soon, in line with corporate strategy. Before that happened, Daniel would make sure he got him into the boat. Bruno would be an important contact, helping him to get the new digital strategy established in the company.

FC Basel had lost, by the way, but that was no longer on his mind.

Happy endings for everyone, every time – hardly feasible

This little episode has a somewhat bitter ending. Not because the local soccer team lost, but because Daniel deliberately builds rapport with Bruno, knowing his company intends to let him go soon. But let's be honest: That is what management practice looks like. It's not always possible to develop employees to a level where they'll be able to add value in the future. Also, asking a few clever questions won't always result in a win-win situation. Leadership tools are used to achieve an overall goal, even if this goal is not in line with the goals of individual people. I decided to let the story of Thomas, Daniel, and Bruno end this way, as it did in real life, so that the use of coaching tools would not appear in an overly idealistic light. Sometimes, opportunism overrides idealism.

With each and every leadership tool, it is up to your personal attitude and leadership ethics to recognize and observe limits in personal interactions. One thing we can give Daniel credit for is that he manages to turn around the negative climate in the company. Bruno comes out of his "basement," feels (and is) needed again, and regains positive energy. For a while, he even bonds with the unloved German colleague, beginning to view him as the technological rebel he himself used to be. The tension fades, the enmity is over, everyone benefits. So does the system. Resources are activated, which, along the lines of the systemic triangle, also has its effects on corporate culture.

Nobody says recognizing situations is easy

Did Daniel choose the right approach when he decided to keep asking Bruno questions and refrain from talking about himself? Or was this a desperate attempt to copy the style of his mentor, Thomas, just like he did when entering the bar? I'll let you be the judge. In any case, it seems Daniel achieved a breakthrough. He managed to base his relationship with Bruno on a new foundation. In his next technical discussion, using coaching tools alone might not get him very far – if it is true that people in the company have no clue as to what digitalization is all about. In which case, Daniel, the visionary, and his people will not be on an equal footing.

Instead, he will need to explain things to them, give advice, be their mentor. In other words, the slider will have to move towards Push quite a bit, since helping people to help themselves won't work here. That said, Daniel can't treat all his people like first-graders. He will need to convince and inspire them. And there will be areas where he can learn from them; for example, how to get approval for IT projects even if there are obstacles in the way. Project management is another area where he won't be able to teach them a lot. But he will have to engage them, get them into the boat, make sure they stay on board, and keep their motivation up. So, everything depends on the particular situation: Managers need to be able to recognize whether in a given situation people need coaching or something else. And they need to adjust the slider to the appropriate position between Push and Pull.

Chapter 5: Takeaways

- As a manager, you have the option to give your people impetus through coaching. In line with the agile leadership approach, however, it depends on the situation as to whether coaching is appropriate. Coaching is not right for every situation.

- In its pure form, coaching means helping people to help themselves. As a coach, you are on an equal footing with the person you coach, and you focus on asking the right questions. That person learns *with* you, not *from* you, then finds the answers on his or her own.
- Coaching is different from mentoring, consulting, training, and teaching, in that it is more about Pull than Push. A coach does not give advice, as a mentor or consultant would, and nor does he or she impart new knowledge, as a teacher would.
- Picture a slider you can move between two end positions, Push and Pull, depending on the situation. Often, you will adjust that slider several times when talking to a person.
- Developing employees so they can make better use of their own resources is an essential contribution to cultural change in your organization. Culture cannot be influenced directly – only indirectly, by pulling other levers.

Chapter 6
Who is coachable? – or:
You can't make pigs fly

Anyone who wants to help people help themselves can coach. By the same token, everyone is basically coachable – but not in every situation! When you have your first flight lesson, your flight instructor will hardly tell you, "Just think what you could do now, so that we can take off." In other words, coaching requires coachees to have the skills and resources they need to help themselves in that particular situation. So, when you want to use coaching tools, you need a kind of situation compass. That is what this chapter is about. You'll see that the "Cautious Performers" are often particularly receptive to coaching guidance. While they often have the capabilities, they tend to need a little push to use those capabilities.

Laura was annoyed. Through the pouring rain, the recruitment consultant had hurried from her office to Frankfurt's main train station. On the way, she had made a reservation for the fast train to Cologne, and all she had gotten was a seat at a table for four. While the train was speeding through hilly landscapes, occasionally dipping into dark tunnels, then shooting out like a bullet, and always swaying vigorously, Laura once again went over the presentation she wanted to give to one of her key clients. The candidates she had found weren't bad, but she would have liked to present someone better. That rankled her. Through the loudspeaker, a voice with a strange accent had just said something about "... our next stop Montabaur ..." and "... connection to Limburg via Dreikirchen and Niedererbach ..." when her iPhone vibrated. Adriano's beaming face appeared, and Laura could see he was wearing his usual attire: a superbly tailored suit with matching tie and handkerchief. The CEO of a Milan-based furniture multinational, no consumer had ever heard of Adriano because he licensed his products to some of the world's most prestigious fashions labels. As a pleasant side-effect of Laura's having maintained this long-standing business contact (and reliable source of referrals – he had given her lots of valuable tips for potential candidates) she was the proud possessor of a floor lamp by Viviane Eastwood and slept in a Ronny Huffinger bed.

"Ciao, Adriano, come stai?" she said cordially, as though she had expected the call. When on the phone with clients, she never let on that she was feeling any stress. She was too much a professional for that.

He did not even bother with a greeting. "Are you craaazy?" his voice boomed from the phone, so loudly that the two passengers opposite her were rolling their eyes. The rant that followed was just as noisy. Over the next five minutes, Laura couldn't get a word in edgewise. When she finally had a chance to respond, she remained calm and fact-based. No, of course she would never give away her sources. Yes, she was awfully sorry that the candidate had called Adriano and called him a "blabber-mouth" and a "walking tabloid." No, she had no explanation for that. Yes, she would take care of this immediately, then call him back.

In Cologne Laura caught a taxi and gave the driver her client's address. "My aunt lives around the corner," the driver said, "You wouldn't believe all the construction that's going on in that district." And she went on to give Laura a detailed account of the current major building sites in Cologne. When she was finally finished, Laura grabbed her phone again and called her office. Ivan, her new assistant, answered. Cheerful and communicative, the young man had made a swift advance in a career at a sales organization, then ended up in a pool of sharks. As he had not been able to stand his ground there, he had resigned. The job at Laura's office seemed perfect for him, although he still had a lot to learn about the field of personnel placement.

"Hey Ivan. Remember that list of names I gave you a couple of days ago, asking you to probe very cautiously to find out whether any of those people were interested in a job change? Was there a Mr. Scarpia on that list?"

"Scarpia? Yes, I called him. He was really nice, only towards the end he acted a bit strange."

"And did he ask you how we knew he was looking?"

"Yeah, he did. How did you know? He was already suspecting Adriano: he actually said, 'It's so cool to have such a big shot as a source!' So I told the guy how close you are with him and several other important people. Puff is part of the trade, they say. I learned my share in sales."

"Let's talk about this tomorrow when I get back, okay? For now, Ivan, please don't call any more of those contacts …"

The minute she hung up, the taxi driver continued her rant about Cologne's construction sites. "That site over there, you see that? I drive by that place 20 times a day – you think I'd ever see anyone working there? Not a soul. Traffic's jammed every single day here 'cause the right lane's been closed for months. I'm so fed up with it!"

Laura took a deep breath, then called Adriano. She took full responsibility for the situation – told him she had given her new assistant free rein in calling up those contacts without briefing him appropriately. That he'd come from another industry and didn't know the ropes yet.

"You have stage 1 person 1 at your office?" Adriano asked, laughing out loud. "I should have figured."

Laura didn't know what he was talking about, although the term sounded familiar. Hadn't Susanne talked about grades like that, from 1 to 4, in one of her seminars? Probably at the last one, "The war for leadership talent" in Shanghai. Laura had been so jet-lagged that she'd dozed off during Susanne's session and later somehow also managed to lose her grandmother's heirloom ring. What a great trip that had been. Not. Laura gritted her teeth. She had been planning to call Susanne, her Hamburg-based coach, anyway. She felt angry with herself for letting this slip-up happen and wondered what Susanne might suggest on what to do about Ivan.

"Nah," the driver said when they got to the destination, and Laura pulled out her credit card, "I only take cash."

Challenged or overwhelmed?

If you are under the impression now that coaching could be your new secret weapon, a weapon you can use anytime, anywhere, to get people to take initiative, let me warn you: It's not like that. Yes, everyone is basically coachable – but not in every situation. You only use coaching tools when the person concerned has the capabilities and resources to help himself or herself. If that person has no way of knowing how something is done, or lacks the self-confidence to develop a solution, coaching is not the right approach. In that case, you move the slider more toward Push, as described in the previous chapter. In other words, you shift to a more directive type of communication. You provide information, or guidance, or you share your own experiences, assuming the mentor role. So, what if the opposite is the case? What if someone is a top performer already, capable of mastering almost anything? Well, in that case let them do their thing and don't get in the way.

Laura, the placement consultant, is feeling stressed out. She makes a mistake and, as a result, gets a very unpleasant phone call. She hasn't taken the time to give her new assistant Ivan a good briefing and properly introduce him to his job. Giving in to the temptation to unload some of the burden, she has delegated a task he's not up to. In Laura's eyes, Ivan is a top performer, and his track record seems to prove it. But he's earned his credentials in another industry – in Laura's field, he's a beginner. He can apply some of the skills he acquired in his old job, but not all of them. I will come back to this point later on. Ivan doesn't know – and cannot know – that headhunters never tell people who referred them to a candidate. Laura should have told her rookie assistant about this iron-clad rule. Ivan may be a top talent, but to master his first challenge – making contact with possible candidates – coaching is not what he needs. Nor has he reached a level of competence that allows him to complete the task all on his own.

Working with the development stages of Situational Leadership

How could Laura have known whether Ivan is coachable in this particular situation? Is there a simple and practical way to verify this for a given person, and quickly? In my view there is one approach which is freely based on Bandura/Blanchard/Hersey et al. The Learning Stages (or Development Stages) model is a a useful and easycompass to work with. I assume you're familiar with the four stages of cognitive learning, according to Albert Bandura et al., or the model of development stages and respective leadership styles, which forms part of Hersey and Blanchards' Situational Leadership. I am aware that Situational Leadership – as with all models – is controversial, but at this point I am not interested in the pros and cons of different leadership theories. All I am saying is that this set of development stages is one possibility – and a very handy one – to quickly identify whether someone in a given situation is coachable or not. According to a Model of Learning Phases that follows Bandura et al., Maslow and others (see box), coaching is appropriate when the person concerned is a Capable but Cautious Performer. At this stage, a person knows that he or she is capable of something but may feel insecure and therefore isn't fully motivated at all times. It is the third of four learning stages.

Likewise, in a Situational Leadership Model based on Hersey and Blanchard, which comprises four stages from 1 to 4, a coachable employee is located at development level 3. The highest level, 4, marks top performers, so-called "Self-Reliant Achievers," to whom you can delegate any kind of task without thinking twice. Stage 2, on the other hand, is the "Disillusioned Learner": A person who, along with guidance on building skills, needs lots of emotional support to develop further. The lowest stage, 1, is called the "Enthusiastic Beginner" – and Laura's assistant Ivan fits that type quite well (as Adriano had recognized). A coachable individual, on the other hand, is at stage 3, the "Cautious Performer": This person is aware that he or she has the basic capabilities, but motivation may be instable, and the person may not really feel up to a task, even if he or she knows how things are done. Often, all it takes is a very slight push to overcome the lack of self-confidence.

> **For those who are coachable: Learning phases and development stages as a compass**
>
> A well-known Learning Phases Model, which is based on the concepts developed by several authors (such Bandura, Maslow etc.), provides a simple and plausible compass to help you decide whether a given employee is coachable or not. The model distinguishes four phases.
>
> - Enthusiastic Beginner ("I am not aware of my inability to complete a task")
> - Disillusioned Learner ("I am aware of my inability to complete a task")
> - Capable but Cautious Perfomer ("I am aware of my ability to complete a task")
> - Top Performer ("I can complete the task without thinking.")
>
> Coaching has its place in the phase of conscious competence. It is only when you know you are capable of completing a task that you will be able to develop a solution, prompted by the right questions.
>
> The enthusiastic beginner on stage 1 needs clear directions from his/her leader. On stage 2 guiding is the right support for

> the person. Between stage2 and stage3, a shift "from telling to asking" takes place. At stage 3, it suffices to help people help themselves. Together, the four stages describe the individual development of an employee. They can also be used as a basis for a development plan you can draw up jointly with the person concerned. This way, you can develop a strong team that will support you effectively and relieves you from some of your workload.

Development stages and competences are always task-specific

Ivan is at stage 4 when it comes to cold calls – a top performer who was among the best in his old workplace. Calling people on the phone and involving them in a deeper conversation – that is something this young man can do in his sleep. Negative experiences can't discourage him, his self-confidence is unshakable. But when it comes to making first contact with a potential placement candidate, Ivan is at stage 1 – a euphoric beginner who has no clue about the potential pitfalls he needs to avoid. And yet, Laura has delegated this task to him. She mistook a stage1 for a stage 4. If you think this is extreme, note that it can be very difficult to assess maturity and development stages correctly – after all, they are always task-specific. To Laura, Ivan seemed like a highly motivated pro. She should have taken a closer look. Every employee goes through different development stages – and they always do so with regard to each specific task. Remember Bruno, the seasoned IT man from the previous chapter? In his time, he introduced the latest technology at the company. Now, as digitalization moves into the next and more advanced stages, he needs to start over from scratch again.

Likewise, people's capabilities and skill levels are related to individual tasks. Ivan brings to Laura's firm lots of skills from his old position. He knows how to make effective phone calls, how to work his way around receptionists and assistants, and how to use storytelling to warm people to an idea. All these things make up his set of transfer skills, which he can use in his new job. However, in his new job he also needs to deal with industry-specific practices and his firm's own rules. This is a kind of skill he can't build on his own. He needs a manager to help him build it.

In my observation, transfer skills tend to be overlooked and underestimated. Often, the simple question "Have you ever done anything like this before?" is never asked. Instead, managers shower people with explanations, ignoring their resources. If you want to take motorcycle driving lessons, a good instructor will begin by asking you whether you have a driver's license for automobiles. If you do, he won't need to start from point zero.

Does all of this sound complicated to you? Welcome to the world of agile leadership! It is complex. It can also be a lot of work.

Dratted third year

Roger, head of sales at a global consumer goods company headquartered in Luxembourg, was happy. The past two days had been just to his liking. As they did every autumn, the 70 top sales executives had met to set the course for the upcoming year. This time, the company had rented an entire first-class hotel on the Cote d'Azur. Built like an Italian palazzo, the hotel was situated on a peninsula and surrounded by an expansive private park. From the large pool, which was lined with old trees and had a view to the sea, several paths and stairways led down to the beach. On the terrace, the restaurant served excellent wines with dinner. Luxurious convertibles had been put at the guests' disposal, so they could end the day by exploring the area. Everything had been organized just perfectly. To top it off, the US business guru Han H. Hirshberg had been flown in for a 30-minute keynote speech. Roger was sure this management retreat would not fail to make an impression. Now he was looking for

Pascale, the HR manager in charge, to congratulate her on her choice of location and express his thanks for the excellent organization. He'd looked at the pool, at the beach, and on the restaurant terrace.

At last he found her in the Midnight Bar, which was located a bit further off towards the garden. The sun was still out, the swing doors were wide open and a warm breeze was gently blowing through the room. Pascale was the only guest. Everyone else was at the pool, the restaurant, or the beach. Or they had taken one of the cars and gone off to Monaco or Nice. Pascale was sitting at a tiny little table at the center of the room. She was wearing black sunglasses and staring into space. An Aperol Splash was on the table before her, half empty. Behind the bar, a bartender in a white jacket and black bow-tie was clearly bored out of his mind.

"Pascale, chère amie, I really want to congratulate you!" Roger effusively greeted his colleague. "These two days have been simply 'parfait'!"

"Merci," Pascale replied dryly. "Thank goodness. Would you believe I had to save the day yet again? I thought I could finally rely on Alain to get it all done. But nothing's changed – in the end it's always me who's stuck with all the last-minute chores."

"Sorry to hear that, ma chère! Do you want to talk about it? How about we take a nice little walk in the park? It's a bit early for the Midnight Bar, don't you think?"

With Roger's full attention and open appreciation, Pascale regained some of her energy. A relaxed little walk with the 62-year-old grandseigneur of sales, who – clad in a blue-and-white Paul and Shark outfit – looked like he had just stepped off a yacht, sounded tempting. Pascale left her drink on the table, and they stepped outside into the sun. A few minutes later, when they were strolling through a narrow cypress-lined alley with a view to the bay of Villefranche-sur-Mer, Roger came back to the issue she had mentioned earlier.

"You feel like talking about Alain?" he asked her. "You can't depend on him, you say?"

"Well, I would have thought he would catch on faster. Three years ago in Dubai, Alain basically spent all day looking over my shoulder. But that was okay, he was new. I took care of everything – everything! – myself. Including the sound check in the auditorium. Alain just watched."

"And last year, when we went to Malta?"

"Well, he did start coordinating some things on his own. But, you know, I do have my standards of how meetings like these should be prepared. I can't stand sloppiness, and I want my people to give me a daily update. When they don't, I go nuts."

"How about this year?"

"I thought he'd be able to do most of it on his own, since he had been with us twice before. I didn't plan to invest so much time again. After all, that's what I hired him for. But then he came asking me what to do about the transfer from the airport. Seriously? After he watched us organize it twice before? I almost lost it! I didn't, thank heavens, just threw him out of my office. That was when I realized he's not making any progress, that I still have to take care of everything myself."

"What could have been the real reason why he asked that?"

"Uhm ... what do you mean? Surely he didn't ask me just for fun."

"No, of course he didn't. But let's assume he did have an idea about how to get 70 managers from the airport to the hotel."

"You think he just wanted reassurance? Sort of like a push because he somehow felt insecure?"

"Could be."

"Roger, can we trade jobs? I think I'm in the wrong place at HR."

"Why would you say something like that, my dear? You just told me all about what Alain needs at this point: a little attention from time to time, but no directives. I'm sure he can organize next year's meeting, and he'll do just fine!"

"Another year, another chance?"

"C'est ça!"

Using coaching to turn cautious performers into top performers

Employees at stage 3– loosely based on the model by Hersey and Blanchard – are on their way to being Top Performers. Coaching tools enable you to facilitate this transition for your people by encouraging them and giving them strength. A typical stage 4 person, although a Cautious Performer with regard to a specific task, is usually far advanced in his or her skills. Unlike a stage 4 individual, however, who is both skilled and highly developed a stage 3 person often lacks commitment. If we assume commitment to be composed of self-confidence and motivation, usually one of the two is lacking. In Alain's case, while he had long since understood how to prepare a sales managers convention, he felt emotionally insecure. That is why he turned to his boss, Pascale, under some random pretext. According to the Process Communication Model® (PCM), Alain is mostly a Harmonizer and Thinker, and he needs a bit of emotional support. Pascale, on the other hand, with strong Promoter-Persister elements fails to understand his motive. She believes Alain has got stuck at stage 2 (or even 1.5), and still needs direction. Due to this misconception, she is so disappointed she kicks him out of her office. The result: Everyone is even tenser, and the stress level rises even higher. Pascale starts resuming tasks that Alain could have easily coped with. So, while the organization of the retreat turns out well in the end, Pascale feels frustrated and empty.

Another option for her would have been to lead Alain with questions, thus helping him to help himself. If she had taken just a few minutes to interact with him instead of throwing him out, she would have been spared a lot of stress and extra work. In my experience, this kind of wrong behavior by managers towards their people – individuals who are actually coachable – happens quite often. Angry words are said, such as "I can't believe you're asking me this!" or "Oh, for heaven's sake. What do you need *now*?" Or, even worse, managers think, "Everything is always left for me to do," swallow their anger, and then sit down with their people to give them directions: "Alright, listen up, this is what you do …" – which is fatal, as stage 3 individuals don't want to be treated like a stage 2 or even stage 1. Roger, on the other hand, does many things right. He communicates with Pascale as an equal. Pascale is one or two management levels below his, but in many areas she's a top performer like himself. Without actually getting involved in her work, Roger dedicates his time and attention to her. With a few good questions, he gets her back on track. He helps her to help herself.

There will never be a point where all staff are top performers

To sum it all up, employees are coachable with regard to a specific task and at a specific point on their learning curve. In a nutshell: They're coachable when they're good at that task but not excellent. An Enthusiastic Beginner (stage 1) would only be confused by coaching questions. This person (willing but not able) needs direction: clear instructions, check lists, and training sessions to build skills. People at stage 1 are not aware of what they don't know. It only dawns on them at the next stage (2), when they turn into Disillusioned Learners. Now they realize how difficult it is to get really good at something. This, by the way, is the stage at which most people stop learning another language or how to play a musical instrument. If you use coaching questions with people at that stage, you risk aggravating them. After all, how would you like it if your French teacher asked you a coaching question? "Can you think of a good way to learn the Conditionnel Passé?" You would probably feel as if he or she was making fun of you. And you would be right. At this stage, what you need is guidance plus emotional support, so you will succeed in building further skills.

Only the Cautious Performer (stage 3) is coachable. This person finds guidance in questions like "What do you feel like doing now?" or "What would your old boss have done in your place?" These questions provide a much-needed push and thus help people find their own solutions. Beware though: You need to be ready for top performers (stage 4) to fall back to stage 3 – for instance, because they are under severe stress momentarily, and their motivation has dropped. Sometimes, even the best people need a little energy from others. Even they can experience emotional crises. Whenever you wonder about odd behavior ("Why is this guy acting so strange now?" or "What made this woman e-mail me in that tone?"), a stress response might be the reason. When a 50-year-old colleague sends me a text message in teenage slang, such as "Hey Masha – what's up? (three smileys)" I assume she just needs some of my attention or energy. Take my advice: Don't be too quick to judge! Test reactions, probe again. A given situation might be just what you think it is – then again, it might not. A member of your team who begs you, "Please tell me what to do" may be an ordinary stage 2 person – or a desperate stage 3. And should you harbor the hope that all your staff will someday be Top Performers, so all you need to do is delegate: Forget it. It's an illusion. For all these reasons, it's a good idea to have a few coaching tools in your repertoire.

Chapter 6: Takeaways

- In principle, anyone is coachable – but not in every situation. Use coaching tools when people have the skills and resources to help themselves, and all they need is a little nudge.
- If you try to coach people who are not ready for it, you'll only confuse or aggravate them. So, make sure you have a compass at hand to assess situations correctly.
- Employees are not Beginners or Top Performers as such. Rather, they are always more or less developed with regard to a certain situation and a specific task. As is the case in agile leadership, the art is in interpreting situations correctly.
- Never underestimate your people's transfer competence, particularly when they come from another organization or industry. Ask them questions such as, "Have you ever done something like this in another job?"
- Don't decide too early what situation you are dealing with. Your first guess may be right, but then again, it might not. Test reactions, dig deeper, find out what this individual really needs from you in this particular situation.

Chapter 7
Making coaching possible – or:
Proper tool application is key

You know now who is coachable. You are aware that an employee can be the solution expert. And you have gotten to know a few coaching tools. So, are we ready to begin? Almost. Or, to be more precise: Under certain conditions. There's something else we need: The right setting. Coaching only works when there is clarity and trust between you and the other person. So, if you want to use coaching tools you need to be ready to listen actively and with empathy. Also, you should check every now and then, by asking the right questions, whether your assumptions and preconceptions really are on target. This chapter deals with these indispensable conditions for the effective application of coaching tools.

"Come in!" Horst called to the person knocking at his office door. The CEO of a manufacturer of digital display columns and electronic access barriers, he was sitting at his desk, sleeves rolled up, and staring at his laptop. Finally, his company had secured a large order from a global company headquartered in nearby Munich. Several of the group's subsidiaries would be equipped with the latest solutions for access and clocking systems. A university-trained engineer in his early fifties, Horst was proud he had managed to outdo scores of competitors. "Integrate, think systems, offer end-to-end solutions," was his mantra. It was also his screen saver: The words would move across the screen in red on black whenever he wasn't using his notebook for longer than five minutes, which didn't happen very often.

"Come in, please!" Horst shouted, louder this time, when nothing happened. Then he looked at the screen again.

Slowly, the door opened and Adile, his chief accountant, hesitantly stepped in. She wore a light summer dress that covered most of her arms, and a headscarf. Silent, she stood in the door frame and looked at Horst questioningly. Was this a bad time? her look said.

"Adile! Come in and have a seat," Horst said, briefly looking up, then back to the screen.

Adile carefully closed the door and sat on one of the visitors' chairs in front of Horst's desk. Through the tilted windows, heavy trucks could be heard thundering by the 1970s-era office building and to a nearby logistics center. For a while, Adile sat there waiting for her boss to interrupt his work.

"What can I do for you?" Horst finally asked in a friendly tone, briefly looking up again, before he went back to staring at his screen. Then he began scrolling through a 300-page document that the new customer had sent them.

"Erm. Well, you know our big move is coming up."

"Right."

"And so me and some other people are beginning to wonder about a few things."

"Such as?"

"One question is, who's is going to share offices with whom."

"Sure."

"I mean, will it be the same as over here, or different? Robert keeps asking me. I understand there's no final decision yet"

"That's correct."

"Well, it looks like the shell of the building is standing and they're starting on the interior work, but no one tells the colleagues where their offices will be and who they will share them with."

"That's unfortunate."

"And no one knows who's in charge of making a floor plan."

"Which is not okay, obviously."

"So, some of the colleagues have started hooking up, like who's going to sit with whom. Don't get me wrong, it's just a suggestion."

"Sounds like a good thing!"

"But no one knows whether that is how it's going to be eventually."

"Right."

"So, should I ask all the colleagues how they would like it to be at the new office building?"

"Good idea!"

"After that, we would have to talk to the architects to see whether it'll work out that way."

"Exactly."

"Surely, the architects will want to know whether our boss has approved."

"Possible."

"So … I could take care of this, if it's alright with you. I get along well with everyone."

"Wonderful, go ahead."

"So it's alright with you?"

"Sure it is!"

Horst went back to staring at the screen, scrolling a bit further down every once in a while. When Adile remained seated, silently staring at her hands, he looked up again and gave her a friendly smile.

"Is there anything else?"

"Thanks ... I guess that would be all for now," Adile replied slowly. But something seemed amiss. She got up hesitantly and walked to the door, when her boss's smartphone started blurting out his ringtone: "We are the Champions." Horst answered the call.

"No, darling, it's not a bad time. I just finished talking to Adile ... Yes, she's just about to leave ... Oh, goodness! ... You're kidding?! ... How about we discuss this over dinner tonight? At Luigi's? ... I really have to tell you about those coaching tools I am working with these days. You know, the ones that Anna recommended to me? Anna, my coach? ... Exactly. ... I just applied the coaching approach to Adile – you know, from Accounting – and helped her find her own solution, just like Anna said. .... Worked well, I think!"

Listen!

Operation was successful, patient died – that could be a headline for Horst's conversation with his chief accountant, Adile. Not everything he does is wrong, mind you. He's open for a conversation. He quickly realizes there's a problem his people can solve alone, no need for a top-down decision. He wants Adile to make a suggestion – which she does, albeit with hesitation, as she is an introverted type of person. But, and this is the point: at the end, Adile obviously feels confused. She feels she's been played for a fool, rather than helped, and is likely to leave her boss's office with even less energy and self-confidence than she felt before. Why? As an attentive reader, you probably know: The problem is the computer. Or, to be more precise: Horst's dedicating much more attention to the document on his screen than he does to Adile. So, while Horst does make some time for her, this time just passes. His actual focus is somewhere else. The conversation happens "on the side." Horst is not mentally present, he barely responds to Adile, he doesn't create a trust-based climate, and during their conversation, neither his facial expression nor his body language show that he is paying attention. And it is true: He doesn't really listen. Horst has heard a few things about coaching tools, but he doesn't really know how to use them.

In this scenario, almost all of the basic conditions for the successful use of coaching tools are missing. Why are conditions so important? Imagine you want to repaint the walls in your basement. You go to the DIY store to get the best paint and equipment: Brushes with natural bristles, rollers with multi-adjustable telescopic rods, the kind of paint container that professionals use, and so on. But then you forget to dust the walls, you don't line the floor with plastic foil, you don't tape the edges, and you work in the semi-dark. How good is the new coat of paint likely to be? Surely it would have been better to spend less money on tools and give more thought to creating the necessary conditions. Even the best tools are of little use when you don't know how to apply them correctly. It is the same with coaching tools.

Active, empathetic listening is an essential condition for coaching

An employee approaches his boss about an issue. What the boss needs to do now is listen actively and with empathy. I assume you don't feel like reading for the umpteenth time how important active listening is. What matters is what happens in practice. Does the boss manage to dedicate ten minutes to the employee's concern? Without instantly offering a solution? Often, the answer is No. A popular shortcut, for instance, is through questions that are solutions in disguise – such as: "Have you thought of xyz?" or "What if you tried xyz?" In my experience, managers usually find it extremely hard to listen for ten minutes without giving even the slightest hint as to what a possible solution might be. While they have understood the concept of active listening intellectually, they are far from putting it into practice. Which is what explains much of Horst's behavior: While he means well with Adile and wants to help her, he can't seem to pull himself away from his laptop even for ten minutes to pay attention to Adile – who, being an introvert, needs some time to get to the point, which makes things worse – so he continues working on other issues on the side. Then, when his wife calls, he intuitively does all the right things. He says he will listen to her problem over dinner, at their favorite Italian place, when they have time for each other. When the conditions are right. So, Horst basically knows how it is done, only he doesn't apply this knowledge consistently.

> **What does it take for coaching to be effective?**
>
> The solution expert is always the coachee. The coach, on the other hand, must ensure that the conditions for a coaching talk are present. Essential elements of a positive framework – which, together, actually make coaching possible – are these:
>
> - Listening actively and empathetically (Am I prepared to dedicate my attention to this?)
> - Building and sustaining trust (Do I have a rapport with the other person?)
> - Asking questions, over and over (Am I sure I correctly understand what the other person is saying?)
>
> The third is particularly tricky, as most people have not learned how to ask enough questions. Often, we only think we have understood something, while we actually – and subconsciously – make assumptions we don't question.

The power of interjections: minor cause, major impact

Perhaps you were a little amused by the way Horst used interjections such as "right," "exactly," "excellent," "great," or "are you kidding?" During the whole conversation with Adile, he doesn't say much more. Used as expressions of sentiment, interjections are not necessarily complete sentences. When Horst, in his talk with Adile, limits his contributions to these interjections, one of the purposes is to entertain you, the reader, as at some point it starts getting funny. The second purpose is to call your attention to the power of interjections. Most of the time, we use them unconsciously. Then we are sometimes surprised by the effect.

Suppose one of your employees comes to you, all enthusiastic, and tells you, "This month looks like we are going to break our sales record!" You can imagine what difference it would make for this person's mood and motivation whether your answer is a booming "Hey – great!" or a weary "Is that right?" Likewise, if you use interjections consciously while listening actively, they can do a lot for you. With each interjection, you share some of your state of mind. Note that emphasis counts just as much as the words. With supportive interjections, you can exert positive influence and facilitate a person's transition to solution mode. You don't have to exaggerate like Horst.

Why don't you observe yourself for a while and identify ten interjections you use frequently. Then, think about how you could use these same interjections more consciously in the future to positively influence discussions. A well-placed "Excellent!" or "Great!" now and then can massively improve the outcome of a conversation.

Drama kings

At the Milan furniture fair, Adriano – the CEO of the Italian furniture company – was in his element. Just like every year. His diary held about three times as many appointments as he could actually handle. His smartphone rang incessantly. At times, he was talking to customers both on the phone and at the stand. He would then switch between conversations so fast, not missing a detail, that his discussion partners usually wouldn't notice. On the morning of the second day at around 11 a.m., Adriano had had around 50 talks at the stand, answered at least as many calls, and felt like he'd had just as many espressos. Someone called to congratulate him on last night's gala, presenting Kurt Lagerhaus's latest furniture collection. His company produced it for Lagerhaus, just like for other designers' home collections. For the following evening, another major premiere was planned, which was why one of the display areas in the spacious stand was shrouded in heavy purple drapes, offering a dramatic and mysterious sight.

Adriano was in the midst of a talk with three Japanese women in black business outfits, when he noticed Luigi rushing towards him, one of his closest staff members. His shirt was wrinkled, he had deep shadows under his eyes, and he was gesticulating as though his breakfast had been half a box of Ritalin.

"Adriano, Adriano!" he shouted to his boss. From his strained voice, Adriano knew immediately that Luigi was truly desperate – which indicated worse than the usual three daily disasters. He quickly walked a few steps toward him, with outstretched arms, stopped before he could knock over the Japanese ladies, who were standing there very erect. Luigi, in turn, fell into Adriano's arms – as Puccini's Mimi in her famous death scene would fall into Rodolfo's. Then, whispering in Adriano's ear, he told him what had happened: His wife had found out about his affair with his assistant, which had been going on for five years now. It had come to light because the repair service had delivered Luigi's secret second smartphone to his house instead of his office. And since Luigi had not been very creative with his PIN, just using his birth date, his wife had read all the salacious WhatsApp messages they had exchanged over the past several months. After a night of marital drama, Luigi was now completely unfit for work. He needed help, right there and then.

"Bene, bene, just listen," Adriano whispered in his ear. "Now's a bad time. I need to get rid of these Japanese ladies first. After that, we'll talk."

In the back of his mind, he frantically thought about where they could find a quiet spot, amid all the hustle and bustle. Then it dawned on him.

"Behind the curtains! Yes, that's what we'll do: We'll use the new Lara Ashbery living room that will be presented tonight. Sit inside, I'll be there in ten minutes max."

The Japanese ladies made a visible effort to keep from laughing at the sight of two Italian men hugging and whispering in each other's ears. Still, after Luigi had disappeared behind the purple curtains, Adriano was able to convince them to place a major order. Then, he hurried to the back of the stand, slipped between the heavy drapes, and found Luigi slumped on the tan sofa with its pink rose pattern. Everything in here looked very British – Adriano's designers had done a splendid job. On a side table with a dark green leather inlay, Adriano saw a pitcher of whisky and several glasses. He poured Luigi a glass, set it on the coffee table, placed a plate of cookies next to it, and sat down on the sofa with him.

"Merda!" he burst out a second later, when he realized that the cookies were plastic and the whisky was cold, stale tea. "I'll be right back."

When Adriano returned from the caterer's booth with coffee, water, sandwiches, and real cookies and sat back down with Luigi in the half-dark niche. Then he did something he never did. He switched off his smartphone.

A trust-based atmosphere as a basis for coaching talks

I've exaggerated a bit about the scene with Adriano and Luigi, but perhaps it helped to make something clear: The present situation can never be an excuse for neglecting an employee who needs help. Even if it seems the worst moment ever to have a confidential talk: Speak to the person and clarify what you can discuss when. And if the setting doesn't permit any privacy, be creative. Think about where you could take the person to talk in peace, at least for a few minutes. An environment that helps establish trust, calm, and concentration is important, in particular when the person has a serious problem and seems emotionally agitated. I don't even want to think about how many employee problems are never solved because bosses send their people away saying, "I can't deal with this right now," or "This is a bad time." It would be so easy for managers to learn and master a simple sentence: "I don't have time now, but ..." (Insert here: in twenty minutes, in two hours, tomorrow morning, etc.).

On the other hand, it's no better – perhaps even worse – to get into a conversation with someone who is in trouble when you don't have the time and can't really concentrate. Trust between managers and their people is essential when applying coaching techniques. And trust doesn't grow on trees. It requires – not solely, but also – an adequate setting where people can relax and open up.

Ensure clarity, rapport, and trust

So, how can you assess whether someone is willing to respond to coaching tools and techniques? Ultimately, it is a question of rapport. When people are so much in sync in terms of body language and emotions that positive, open, and stress-free communication is possible, we speak of them as having a rapport. The more you need someone to trust you and open up to you, the more rapport you need. You've probably heard of the phenomenon called mirroring. You reach for a glass of water – your counterpart does the same. Then your counterpart assumes a more relaxed position – you automatically do the same. In a healthy conversation, the people involved alternate taking the lead in this kind of body language mirroring. You may want to imitate your colleague's movements very slightly, just once – making sure you don't mimic him or her! – to test or enhance rapport. Begin by watching out for the numerous little body signals: Is there any rapport yet?

A coaching talk is always also about emotions, never about facts only. That's why rapport is so important. You can enhance it using interjections – which I've described at the beginning of this chapter – or by mirroring body language. Another factor that is essential for rapport is your inner clarity. Are your thoughts spinning around in circles? Or are you fully focused on your counterpart and the issue at hand, ready to absorb this person's emotions? It may not show on your face what you're really thinking, but let me assure you: Most people can sense whether you are giving them your full attention or allowing your mind to wander. Why not go ahead and try this out in a conversation about lighter topics – say, the next time you are having small talk. You might just realize that the energy level goes down and the connection to your counterpart starts fading. So, in a trustful setting, it's not enough to find the right words and to mirror the other person's body language – it's important to stay mentally focused, too.

Putting it right

Very carefully, Henry hit the golf ball one last time with his putter. A gusty, almost stormy wind was sweeping the Royal Golf Course in Dublin, with not a single tree and hardly a shrub to ward off the forces of nature. James followed the ball with his eyes. Would his golf partner do it yet again? Yes: The ball disappeared in the hole. Another perfect putt.

"Outstanding, mate!" James said, not without a hint of envy.

"The wind helped," Henry modestly replied.

Henry and James went back many years, having grown up together in a workers' district in Dublin. Now they were both investment bankers, working at a large Irish bank. At the end of the year, James always had the better numbers to show. Henry, for his part, was better at golf. On Saturday mornings, they would meet on the golf course, in every weather. Nothing short of a tornado or heavy snow could stop them – two weather phenomena not too common in Ireland.

"Jill is doing pretty well," James said as they were pulling their trolleys to the next hole.

"Yes, I'm truly happy about her. And a bit proud, of course."

"Proud? It's not like she owes her development to you."

"Come on. You can't say I was never there for her when she needed me."

"Oh, I think it's quite understandable you don't feel like looking after her all the time. She can be a handful, no doubt."

"That's normal at her age."

"She's not *that* young."

"Yeah, we've got the worst behind us, that's true."

"Oh yes, she was quite a bit of trouble at first."

"You're exaggerating. Nothing out of the ordinary."

"But she's got quite independent lately."

"Yeah, you could say that. I'm pleased you noticed."

"She's taking responsibility."

"Well, I wouldn't really call it responsibility. But she has her reasonable moments, no doubt."

"What do you think, how far can she get?"

"Oh, I'm not getting involved in that. She'll have to find out for herself someday, when she's ready."

"Someday? You can' be serious? In times like these, it's never too early to find and promote talent."

"She seems to have quite a musical talent."

"Since when are you interested in that kind of thing?"

"James, come now! I'm a banker, that doesn't make me a dimwit."

"Me, I've noticed a few other things about Jill."

"Such as?"

"Well, she's ... quite attractive. Don't you think?"

"Jill? My Jill?"

"What do you mean, 'your' Jill? She's just as much 'my' Jill."

"Have you gone mad?"

"Hey – no reason to get upset. Political correctness is all nice and dandy – but can't a man say that he finds a woman attractive?" *

"What woman?"

"Well..., Jill."

"You can't be serious. Our little girl?"

"I'm talking about our intern."

"Ah – yes, right. Our intern. Sorry. I thought you were talking about my daughter."

How we forgot how to ask questions – and why we should relearn it

When James talks about Jill's development, Henry could simply ask him which Jill he's talking about. He doesn't. Instead, he instantly assumes James is talking about his daughter. Probably because she's the first person that comes to mind when he hears the name. And when Henry's words seem less and less fitting for the bank intern, James doesn't back-check either. "Are we talking about the same person?" This hesitation to check whether things are really as clear as they seem is typical of adults in our culture. Why is that? Let's go back to Henry's childhood for a moment. Little Henry, lying in a baby stroller that is being pushed by a giant. He sees a black shadow crossing the sky – the giant shouts, "bird!" Little Henry doesn't understand. Later, after he's learned to talk, he can ask: "What's this?" He gets positive feedback because he asks nicely and gets lots of answers. So, he asks more questions and gets more answers. At some point, he doesn't only ask "What?" but also "Why?" The giant strives to provide good answers. Until, at some point, she starts getting annoyed. She says, "Stop asking so many questions, darling!" Or, in a sharper tone, "Stop asking those silly questions!"

At this point, little Henry learns something: Asking too many questions is bad. Perhaps he even learns that only stupid people ask lots of questions. Even when parents never say, "Don't ask so much," children sense when grown-ups dislike a barrage of questions. So, what does little Henry do? He starts making up his own interpretations instead of asking. Later on, as an adult, Henry does the same thing. Unfortunately, however, as adults we keep getting in trouble for making up our own interpretations and projections instead of asking questions. The only thing that helps is relearning how to ask questions. Above all, open questions – questions that cannot be answered with Yes or No. They are essential for successful communication. If you want to apply coaching techniques, one of the indispensable elements you'll need is regular questions, to make sure you've understood the other person correctly. While doing this, it is important to observe different cultural contexts.

It's almost impossible to ask too often whether you've understood correctly

In our cultural environment, almost all of us were brought up with an unfortunate tendency to think up the plot of a story rather than ask those involved what really happened. Probing and revisiting an issue several times to ask again feels awkward to us – while imagining or fantasizing is something we can do on our own, discreetly. So, when in doubt, we prefer to imagine what happened or will happen. What helps us do so are our unspoken convictions and assumptions – which often stem from our past and are connected to our psychological scars. With too many things, we are convinced that they have to be the way we think they are. So, we never ask. In my seminars, I often use the following riddle (which you may have heard before):

Romeo and Juliet are lying on the floor, dead, in a puddle of water. There are shards of glass everywhere. What happened?

I encourage participants to find out by asking open questions. Those that don't know the solution usually offer the wildest theories of how Romeo and Juliet died. So far, nobody has ever asked who Romeo and Juliet are. Well, to cut to the chase, Romeo and Juliet are goldfish and their bowl has fallen onto the floor and shattered to pieces. Nobody ever asks who Romeo and Juliet are because everyone believes they know. Even worse, when someone asks who Romeo and Juliet are, they fear it might appear as though they'd never heard of Shakespeare's play. That would be embarrassing. So they feel it's better not to ask.

Years ago, when not every car had a navigation system, I was driving back to the airport in Switzerland one day to return my rental car and board a plane. When I asked locals for directions to the airport, I was told to follow the signs to the highway. I followed the blue signs, and it took me a whole hour for what would normally take ten minutes, because I kept going around in circles. You've probably guessed why: I didn't know the highway signs in Switzerland are green, not blue like in Austria and Germany. I hadn't thought of asking what the highway signs look like and, as a result, nearly missed my plane. If you want to adopt an attitude where coaching is possible because there is trust, rapport, and clarity – both inner clarity and factual clarity – it's almost impossible to ask too many questions. You should learn not to take anything for granted and to watch out for your own tacit assumptions and projections. And don't forget there are different contexts in different cultures. You can always think of Romeo and Juliet, if you find that helpful.

Finally, a piece of advice: If you know you're dealing with a Harmonizer according to the PCM® model, make sure not to bombard that person with questions. Instead, find a good balance of listening, talking, and asking questions. Otherwise, you'll subject a Harmonizer to considerable stress.

Chapter 7: Takeaways

- There is a set of indispensable basic elements that enables you to use coaching tools effectively. When the framework isn't right, even the best tool won't work.
- Active and empathetic listening is an essential prerequisite for a successful coaching talk. You can't use coaching tools effectively if your mind is elsewhere.
- Brief interjections are an effective and frequently underestimated element of active listening. They allow you to communicate some of your emotions and give the other person encouragement and reassurance.
- Trust-based conversations require a setting where there can be rapport and openness. So, choose your locations carefully. If you or the other person are experiencing stress, it's better to postpone the session by 20 minutes.
- Learn to ask lots of open questions – more than you're accustomed to. To grasp a situation correctly, we need to free ourselves of unconscious assumptions and projections. The only thing that helps here is to ask, listen, ask, and listen.

Chapter 8
Finding solutions – or:
When people don't know what they know

Coachees are their own solution experts – there is broad consensus on this in the coaching community. What a bold statement! And yet, experience has shown that it is definitely possible to guide people towards developing their own solutions. As long as you make sure you are dealing with someone coachable and that the setting is right, sooner or later you will be able to watch – almost as you would in a science lab – how an experiment, with the proper setup, will produce the desired result. People always know much more than they are aware of. That is something you can rely on. And this is why, with courage and creativity, you can help your people solve their own problems themselves.

Curt was sitting at the desk of his tiny office on the top floor of the Bellevue Resort and Spa, a five-star wellness hotel. All the larger rooms in the floors below were guest rooms and suites, which left nothing but the attic for him, the hotel manager. But there was one major advantage to this that made up for having to use this dark, cramped room as an office: When he looked up from his desk and peeked through the small window to his right, he had the most gorgeous view – across Lake Thun to the three peaks of Eiger, Mönch, and Jungfrau, and to the Blümlisalp, a heavily glaciered mountain range. After almost five years in his job, he still couldn't get enough of this view: the turquoise glimmer of the water, the lush green meadows, and the pure white of the snow, which would take on a slight pink glow at dusk.

On this early September morning, however, Curt didn't have an eye for nature's beauty. Frowning, he leafed through a stack of carefully arranged printouts on his desk: Guest reviews from several online booking platforms. On the other side of the desk,

Hans Mayer, the Food & Beverage Manager, was sitting in silence.

"I had just gone to sleep when I was woken by someone yelling in the hallway," Curt read in a flat voice. "Apparently someone from staff – three exclamation marks. How is it possible that someone who works in a wellness hotel – three exclamation marks – a place dedicated to relaxation – two exclamation marks – is shouting in the hallway at night – question mark. I got up and opened the door, and three doors down I saw a young man from room service and an older man in a dark suit – open parenthesis – his supervisor – question mark – yelling at him …"

Over the rim of his reading glasses, Curt briefly glanced at Hans. Hans returned the glance, not moving a muscle. Curt leafed through some more printouts, occasionally reading a sentence or two. "Our little one ran from the dining room crying because one of the waiters yelled at another. … So much for 'an oasis of tranquility': Service staff that yell at each other all day. … On the terrace, someone kept yelling at the waiters. Outrageous – exclamation mark. … I booked a wellness vacation, not primal scream therapy. … Eerie atmosphere, restaurant staff seem frightened, boss keeps yelling at them. … Restaurant manager is a bully. It was embarrassing to watch …"

There was a long pause, during which Hans kept silent.

"Hans," Curt said in a quiet voice, taking off his reading glasses and looking the other man in the eye, "Is it possible at all that these comments by our guests refer to you?"

"Yes, I suppose that would be me," Hans replied.

"And would you say these reviews are to the point? Or are they all wrong?"

"It's true that I do raise my voice sometimes …"

"May I ask why you raise your voice so much?"

Chapter 8: Finding solutions – or: When people don't know what they know

"Well, sometimes you need to tell people loud and clear how things should be done. We're a first-class hotel! Some of them seem to think we're a youth hostel. It's a shame sometimes."

"How familiar are you with modern forms of employee dialog?"

"This is the hospitality sector! I got my share of rebukes myself when I was an apprentice. It didn't do me any harm that my supervisors talked straight with me. Plus, I would have hardly made F&B Manager if I hadn't been straight with people. If I don't yell a bit every now and then, they don't listen."

"How can you tell if someone listens?"

"When they do what I say."

"I see. ... Is there anyone you never yell at?"

"Of course there is. Quite a few, actually."

"What's different about them?"

"I'm relaxed around them."

"These people you *don't* yell at – how often do they follow your orders?"

"Almost always."

"I see. So, what could you do to be this relaxed all day long?"

"I guess I need to do something about being stressed out all the time. I could definitely do with some wellness myself."

"Well, what are you waiting for? You're working at a wellness hotel!"

"You're kidding, right?""

"Not at all, Hans. You know I use the pool every morning, and get a massage once a week or so. And I encourage all our other managers to do the same: Start out the day in peace and serenity."

"To be honest, I've always envied you for your morning swim in the thermal pool."

"Well, why don't you join me, then? Tomorrow morning at 5:15? I'll be there."

All the rage is gone

How do you trigger a solution with a person who you feel has more knowledge and capabilities than what his or her behavior currently indicates? Curt, the hotel director, remains very calm when talking to Hans, the "shouter." He creates a trust-based atmosphere for their talk. Instead of making accusations, he confronts him with third-party feedback. He focuses on clarification, not judgment. You, obviously, are free to choose your own words and messages – but Curt's approach is a good model to follow. He wants the facts on the table, so he starts with a reality check: Is this feedback correct, or is everyone wrong? It is only after Hans has confirmed that the guest reviews refer to him and his behavior has been described accurately that Curt very patiently begins to trigger the problem-solving process with Hans. He mostly uses open questions and interjections, and he listens actively and remains very calm as Hans gets more and more upset. When, finally, Hans realizes that his shouting can't be blamed on a lack of commitment in the people around him but is, in fact, a reflection of his own stress pattern, his boss helps him identify a way to get through the day in a much more relaxed mood. At the end, Curt expedites things by making a concrete suggestion – also because he knows that his colleague wouldn't dare suggest he might join him in his early morning routine.

If you deal with a Persister, be just as persistent!

I only had a few hotel managers as coaching clients so far. But I've certainly worked with quite some people that tended to get loud – a phenomenon you find in all business sectors. In the Process Communication Model® (PCM), they are often people with a strong Persister element. This personality type initially tends to believe they are justified in yelling at their staff. You may need some patience to apply coaching questions productively. A smart person under stress is often quite adept at giving reason after reason why he or she just *has to* act that way. In your role as a coach, what you need at this point is a question that will activate the other person's inner solution energy. A way to put an end to permanent arguing and rationalizing, to clear the path for something constructive to happen. You want that person to take the other door, not the usual one. In Curt's conversation with Hans, the key questions that helped identify a solution are whether Hans yells at *all* his staff and, if not, what's different about the people he doesn't yell at.

This is the point when the penny drops, as the English say (or the proverbial lightbulb goes on). Hans notices that his usual formula "not listening = disobeying" is actually something he has just made up. Listening to someone is not the same as following the rules someone has set. Hans has made up this equation simply to justify his own stress pattern, both to himself and to others. What made him act that way? We can't know from the conversation between the two. In the real-life cases that I've experienced and that inspired me to write this scene, a key reason was that shouting at someone who supposedly wasn't listening was a common behavioral pattern in the person's family of origin. A manager yelling at his staff might have been brought up by a father who believed listening and obeying were the same thing. I mention this here to highlight that, when you use coaching tools, you may come across very old and long-standing behavioral patterns. But that shouldn't discourage you. As long as you stay in your role – listening, asking questions, showing appreciation for your counterpart, and letting him/her identify solutions for themselves – you'll be on the safe side.

We could and we would – but we lack the courage ...

All of us have values and convictions that allow us to do some things with ease while other things are a challenge. The latter can be difficult for others to understand. Our entrenched beliefs go back to our childhood and youth. Many, if not most of them, stay with us for the rest of our lives. As a manager, make sure you don't take your own values and beliefs as the measure of all things. Even when it's quite obvious that people are standing in their own way, their beliefs are never "wrong." They were born from good intentions once and may have served that person well in previous stages of his or her life. And while it may be true that these values and beliefs are no longer helpful, that is something people need to realize for themselves. You can't force it on them. In this day and age, with people from various cultures working on global virtual teams, it's more important than ever before that managers show respect for people's beliefs, however strange they might seem to them.

Values and beliefs are not always the nub of the matter, though. Sometimes the problem is external conditions – or simply biology, as the next story will show. Even with a "shouter," biorhythm can be part of the problem. Hans, the F&B Manager, yelled at his room service people at night – although he must know that guests expect peace and quiet at such a late hour. Who knows, perhaps he's a morning person, and his batteries are empty after a long day. When our energy level is low, we sometimes tend to fall back into old patterns that we have long since overcome in our energetic phases. As a manager, you can help your people take good care of themselves. And if someone acts up because their batteries are low, they need to enhance their own energy management. In situations like these, sometimes a simple question like, "What would it take for you to feel better right now?" can work wonders.

Bedtime stories and escapades

Sandra felt extremely embarrassed. The 30-year-old banker was sitting on a sofa in the small, sun-filled waiting area in her coach Susanne's Hamburg practice. Ivan, her Significant Other, had driven her here from Frankfurt. He was sitting beside her, holding her hand. Ivan's boss Laura, the placement coach, thought highly of Susanne and had warmly recommended her. More than anything, Sandra was happy to be in another city where no one knew her. Susanne came ambling in, right on time and in good spirits.

"Hi there, how are you? Glad you've made it. Would you come next door with me?"

"Is it okay if Ivan comes along?" Sandra asked.

"Sure. This way."

In the other room, Sandra and Ivan sat down exactly the same way as before. Ivan reached for her hand again. After a few welcoming words, Susanne turned to Sandra and asked what she could do for her.

"She has trouble getting out of bed, and she's always late for work. Her colleagues all crack jokes about her." This was Ivan answering.

"I see. But I need you to let Sandra speak for herself, Ivan." Susanne told him, still in the same friendly tone.

"That's alright, Ivan means well, he just wants to make things easier for me," Sandra said. "He's worried. And it's exactly like he said. I set the alarm every morning, sometimes I'm even awake before it goes off, and still I can't get myself to get out of bed. Ivan usually gets up at six and goes for a run. When he gets back, he takes a shower, has an energy bar for breakfast, and drives off to his office. When I'm still in bed when he leaves, I feel completely useless. Sometimes he calls me from the car to ask whether I managed to get out of bed. It's all very embarrassing."

"And how are things at the office?"

"I often get there at 10.15, sometimes even 10:30. My colleagues give me strange looks, but I ignore it. I know they talk behind my back, though. Call me sleepy-head, things like that."

"What does it do to your work when you get there later?"

"Nothing … It's only nine in London when it's ten over here, and nighttime in New York. We work in the back-office, managing family offices' affairs, no client contact. For three years straight, I've been the one to generate the highest average returns in my department, so nobody can give me a hard time. But I do feel bad when I get to work that late."

"How does it feel to you to stay in bed late?"

"Well, as soon as I'm awake I turn on the radio and I think: Just two songs. Then it's another song. Then the news. Then I tell myself: Just this one song, and I'll get up. But I still don't manage. I don't understand why."

"Tell me: How old is the Sandra who stays in bed and listens to some more music?"

"What do you mean …?"

"Just tell me how it feels, without thinking too much."

"That Sandra? I guess she's about 14. She doesn't feel like getting up and going to school. I hated school."

"We are all younger versions of ourselves sometimes, children one day and teenagers the next. In some situations, these younger versions of ourselves can take control. That's completely natural. So, if you judge your inner teenager in your adult mind, you only make things worse. Another way to deal with this is to acknowledge that 14-year-old Sandra and her needs. Right now, I'd like to ask adult Sandra: What time would be okay for you to get to the office? And what could you do to achieve that target?"

"If I managed to get there by nine, no one would give me funny looks. How could I achieve that? A large coffee does help me get into gear. So, if Ivan could bring me a coffee in bed …"

"I'd be happy to do that, sweetie," Ivan was quick to assure her. "All you need to do is tell me."

"Wonderful!" Susanne said. "So, how could we help satisfy some of 14-year-old Sandra's needs, other than listen to music in bed?"

"Well … it would be great if my weekends weren't that crammed with appointments and plans. We never have time to do something spontaneous," Sandra replied.

"We should go back to taking weekend trips at the spur of the moment, like we used to do," Ivan suggested. "We've become pretty boring."

"Yeah, you could say that," Sandra agreed, laughing.

When a younger version of ourselves takes control

Intuitively, most adults know that they sometimes behave like children or teenagers, even when they've never heard terms like "the inner child" or "inner adolescent." Professional life is no exception. On the contrary: Some managers complain about feeling "like being in a kindergarten" when they are with staff. There's a grain of truth there. Everyone brings a younger version of himself or herself to work every day. When under stress, this younger version may suddenly take over – especially when there's a trigger that, subconsciously, evokes situations in that person's childhood or adolescence.

Managers are very wrong, however, in thinking they are the only adults in the kindergarten. *Everyone* has their younger versions with them, including the boss. Besides, it's not very helpful for people development to tell someone they're acting like a child or teenager. On the contrary. It's better to play along and engage with people emotionally. When the intellect judges a person's emotional needs, solution energy is blocked. By adopting a benign-to-neutral attitude about people's "un-adult" behavior, you enable them to acknowledge the needs of their younger selves – which have taken over momentarily – then come back to their adult roles.

Letting people find solutions that expand their room to maneuver

What makes us adults? We live autonomously, we take care of ourselves, and can choose what attitude we want to adopt about a situation. When Sandra wasn't able to get out of bed in the morning, she had lost this sense of self-determination and freedom. She feels embarrassed both to herself and in front of others because of the way she acts – but she doesn't seem capable of changing it. What the coaching talk does, essentially, is give her back her adult freedom. To use it, she needs to acknowledge the 14-year-old Sandra inside her who is claiming her rightful place. She does have all the answers, only her shame and judgmental intellect have been blocking the path to a solution, as fallen trees would block an alley. That is why Susanne, as her coach, only needs to ask a few questions to clear the way. She offers Sandra a safe environment to talk about her problem. Her partner is with her, supporting her emotionally. In itself, this setting activates solution energy.

Sandra knows very well what time she – the adult Sandra – would like to get to the office and what could help her achieve that. Nobody has to tell her. What she needs is a push to do two things: Remember at all times that she is an adult, capable of making decisions, and create the space she needs to feel well. When the alarm goes off in the morning, she can ask herself: Okay, so how old am I? 14 or 30? If I am 30, what is it I want right now? The answer could be something like: "I want a coffee, then gradually get into gear, arrive at the office at around 9, then do a job I like and that I'm good at." If 14-year-old Sandra then asks, "What about me?", adult Sandra may tell her something like: "You can listen to your music while I'm drinking my coffee. And on the weekends, you can have your way. But right now at this moment, I decide to live my adult life."

Just a few more questions

Sitting in her Porsche convertible, Clara nervously played with the push buttons in the center console. She had decided to take the highway, which was a small detour, to get from her Cascais home to her office in the old town of Lisbon , hoping it would be faster that way and she would make it on time. Now she was stuck in a traffic jam, at a total standstill. All around the city, every single road was jammed. Her father would be at the office long before her, awaiting her all calm and relaxed, and she would be late for their appointment. Again! Clara was stressed out, and she knew one thing for sure: No way would she be able to switch to a state of meditative serenity, just like that, like some Indian fakir. Officially, it had been two years now since 37-year-old Clara became general manager of the real estate investment firm her father had established over four decades ago. But the truth was, the old man was still around, and very present. He was the first to arrive in the morning, and he would often still be at his desk in the evenings when Clara had long since gone home to look after her family. The senior boss was intimately familiar with the old boys' network in Portugal's political circles. He played golf with the billionaires that lent his firm their money to see it grow. *He* was still the firm – not Clara.

For months, Clara's dinner talks with her husband Bernardo had centered around that subject. Bernardo thought Clara should put her foot down and show her old man who was the boss now.

He had no idea! If she acted like a stubborn child, insisting that she was the boss now, she'd only embarrass herself. Today was another one of those days when Clara urgently needed her father's advice. That was why they had agreed to meet at 10 a.m. The company was planning to build Europe's largest outlet center – nothing less – on the fringes of the Ruhr industrial region. It would involve a highly complex mezzanine financing structure with a gazillion potential pitfalls. Negotiations with the banks were scheduled for the following week. Clara's father had always been known for his high equity ratio, which was one of the things his business partners valued about him. But then again, they shouldn't push the envelope. Clara had mixed feelings about this.

When at last she stepped into her father's office on the principal floor of a stately old villa, it was 10:25. The old man was sitting at his desk, absorbed in the local newspaper. He didn't even look up when Clara gave him a dramatic account of the traffic jam. She sat down in one of the heavy old armchairs adorned with wooden carvings and began to outline the strategy she wanted to pursue in the negotiations with the banks. Her father instantly put down his paper and listened carefully.

"So, Papa," Clara finally said, "I'm going to need a decision before the end of this week. Should I go forward with this – or not?"

"I've understood your strategy," the old man replied, "and I'll tell you what I think of it in a minute. But before I do that, let me ask you a few questions."

If you are unsure whether or not someone has the answer

What would you do if you were in the senior company owner's place? Tell your daughter how to approach such a major project? Let her go ahead? It's not a trivial decision to make. A lot of money is at stake, and there are more than a few risks, too. The old man isn't entirely sure whether his daughter is up to the challenge and struggling to find the courage. Or whether she lacks the experience to handle a financing plan of this magnitude. At that point, the old fox uses a little trick: He tells her he will give her the advice she seeks. His daughter is used to getting directions from her father whenever the going gets tough, so he knows he can't simply tell her that this must stop. In other words, he acknowledges Clara's need for guidance, which is extremely important. He is perfectly willing to give her that guidance, too, but he isn't sure whether she really needs it. He senses that she's finally ready to fill the role of general manager. He's also aware that it is time for him to step back. But is Clara ready?

To find out, the old man does a loop: He says, "I'll give you my opinion in a minute. But before I do, I'll ask you a few questions." These coaching questions will help him find out where Clara is standing. For instance, he might address a few particularly sensitive points in the financing plan and ask her how she intends to handle them. He might ask her what she thinks of the whole project, and where she sees analogies and differences with the company's existing and previous projects. With a few good questions, Clara's father can find out whether Clara has all the answers and simply needs reassurance – or whether he, the more experienced of the two, should insist on having the final say in this important matter. After he has asked all his questions, the conversation will arrive at a decision-making point: Either the questions and answers have helped clarify things – in that case, Clara may even forget to remind her father that she wanted his opinion. Or it will be obvious that a decision is needed from him because Clara's not ready yet and has realized this. In that case, it is important that the old boss deliver on his promise and give his daughter his opinion, plus some advice; if need be, he might even make the decision himself. In essence, what a leader does in this situation is move the slider between Push and Pull.

> **Three-step technique for cases of doubt**
>
> Let's assume one of your people comes to you looking for guidance, as usual. How do you find out whether this person has the answers already? Or whether they really need an answer from you? This three-step conversation technique can help.
>
> **Step 1:** You acknowledge the person's request for guidance and tell him or her you'll state your opinion in a minute.
>
> **Step 2:** You get the person's okay for asking a few questions ("Can I ask a few questions first?") and use coaching questions to clarify where they are really standing.
>
> **Step 3:** Depending on the outcome of step 2, you either a) let the person find a solution or b) make good on your promise and tell them your opinion or provide guidance.
>
> Be sure to use the words "May I ask a few questions first?" or "Let me begin by asking a few questions " (or something like that) as this helps to interrupt the chain of cause-and-effect and to get the person out of their usual expectation that you will have the answer.

Self-observation helps to assess others correctly

Nobody is a top performer in all spheres of life. Nobody is even close. And there's no need to be an expert in everything. In a highly specialized society, it's easier to live with deficiencies since there are always others who are better at certain things and have greater interest in them. Some people might say: I can cook well enough to put a tasty and healthy meal on the table for my family anytime. That's as far as my ambitions go. I don't need a cooking class with a star chef, or a cooking coach. The more frequently and the more thoroughly we think about where – in which areas of life – we are at stage 1, 2, 3 or 4 (see Chapter 6), the more reliably we can assess others. To apply coaching techniques successfully, it's particularly important to know who is at the coachable stage 3.

If you are realistic, you'll know that you can fall back from stage 4 to stage 3 at any point. Which is not a problem at all. On the contrary, it can help enhance your understanding of others. I was in that situation, for instance, when I first gave one of my seminars in English – to native speakers. I had given seminars in English for years, and it never occurred to me this could be a problem. But the group had never been made up of native speakers. The prospect of having to speak English in front of natives initially blocked me. Well, worse things can happen. I needed a moment, then I realized nothing would be different. Sometimes we've done things before, but not in a specific context – which can temporarily unnerve us. The more self-reflected you are when that happens, the better you can help yourself. Or help others help themselves.

Chapter 8: Takeaways

- Triggering the solution-finding process in someone you're quite sure has all the answers – that's basically what you do when you apply coaching tools in people development.
- In particular, when you deal with Persisters (according to the PCM® model), you may need a lot of patience. Hang on until you've managed to put an end to stubborn arguing and rationalizing, so that their own "solution energy" can emerge and unfold.
- Our long-standing values and convictions, all the patterns we've acquired in our childhood and youth, can get in the way of our further development. Remain patient and try not to push people too hard. They need to realize of their own accord where old patterns are no longer helpful.
- We all carry younger versions of ourselves inside us: Our inner child and our inner teenager. Sometimes these younger selves take over. When we notice that, we can use coaching questions to help ourselves and others make adult decisions and regain our freedom.
- If you are not sure whether a person actually has all the answers, offer them your help but begin by asking coaching questions. With the help of these questions, you can clarify whether people actually need your help or can help themselves.

Chapter 9
Tools and techniques – or:
No matter what I use, it will work!

There are lots of coaching tools and techniques. Nearly all of them are legitimate and work beautifully. So, it doesn't really matter which one of them you use. It's almost like when you want to draw a portrait: Whether you use a pencil or charcoal – or a computer mouse – the outcome will still be a portrait. You can even use a pen or carve the portrait into a wooden board with a knife. In that sense, the three tools described in this chapter are just suggestions. You know by now how best to approach a coaching situation: Build resonance, listen empathetically, ask attentive questions, help others find their own solutions. The key is your inner attitude, the matching framework, and moving the slider back and forth between Push and Pull.

The palace-like building near Ringstrasse in Vienna was notorious for its endless and sparsely lit hallways. It was the seat of the Society for the Promotion of Digitalization and Automation. Egon Pilcher, the president, had decided one day – on his sixtieth birthday, to be exact – that he would never again run down those long and dark hallways, even if he was in a hurry. Ever since then, his staff had been unable to observe whether he was stressed out or had plenty of time. On this Wednesday morning, Egon – who had a penchant for light-colored suits and bow-ties – was ambling down the hallway, at a pace as leisurely as if he were on a Sunday afternoon stroll in the park.

"Mr. Pilcher, Mr. Pilcher," a voice sounded through the hallway. It was Karl, formerly the head custodian, now the facility manager. Waving both his arms, his face a deep red, he was storming towards Egon. "It's so good to find you here! I'm at the end of my tether. Everyone complains to me because some of our coffee machines are out of coffee. But I'm not responsible for that, just for machine maintenance!"

"Listening to you like that," Egon calmly replied, "I really feel like having a cup. How about discussing this on the scene, so to speak? I mean, in that coffee area over there? Perhaps we'll find a solution there."

Karl agreed and followed Egon. In the coffee nook, Egon reached for a cup, set it down below the spout, and pressed the mocha button. Nothing happened.

"What would be an ideal coffee situation for you?" he asked the facility manager.

"I don't want to hear any more complaints!" Karl heatedly replied. "And, well, it would be good to have enough coffee here for everyone at any time."

"I see," Egon said, pressing the button once again. When nothing happened, he hit the side of the machine with his flat hand. Nothing. "So, what's the reason we don't have this situation here at the moment?"

"Well, every hallway wants something else: Some want Meinl, others Lavazza, others want the coffee from the café across the street. That's why they all buy their own coffee and fill it in the machine. I don't mind that – let them drink what they want. But don't come complaining to me when we're out of coffee!"

"This can't go on like this!", Egon replied, once again pressing the mocha button while simultaneously hitting the side of the machine with his other hand. The cup remained empty. "What other ways do we have to establish a satisfactory coffee situation?"

"Well, there are vendors for this kind of thing. Coffee Service Haferl, for example. They could come and refill our machines every day. But then people would have to drink what's there."

"What do you think would be a good solution?"

"Perhaps we could use two vendors, so we wouldn't have to depend on one only."

"Excellent idea!" Egon made a fist with his right hand and hit the mocha button with full force. The commotion made the cup slide off the machine. It fell to the ground and broke into several pieces.

"Leave it there, Mr. Pilcher! I'll clean this up in a minute."

"Yes, thank you … Sorry about that! So, what are you going to do? And do you need anything else from me?"

"Well, since I put up the machines here, I can decide what coffee we use. So far, I've let people make their individual choices, but that didn't work. So, what I'll do now is I'll write an e-mail to say that I am thinking about a vendor, and ask them for suggestions on a possible billing mode."

"Very well, go ahead and do that," Egon said. He wished Karl a nice day and walked back to his office. He had forgotten where he had originally been heading.

Karl put a fresh cup under the spout, pressed the button briefly, but with force, waited for the cup to fill up, and went back to his vestibule office for his coffee break.

Grow and go

Several stories in this book have demonstrated how to guide staff members towards a solution by asking open questions. You don't necessarily need to master specific questioning techniques – as long as you stick to the iron-clad rule of not pre-empting the solution. In essence, you use what Socrates, the ancient Greek philosopher, referred to as "midwifery": You use patient and persistent questioning to support the birth of ideas and solutions.

You enable your counterparts to come up with their own solutions. The previous chapters have outlined the prerequisites, so I could have ended this book after Chapter 8. The following sections offer some more details, which I hope you will find useful as well. In this present chapter, I'll introduce three very handy tools you can use in your daily management routine: the GROW or TO-GROW model according to John Whitmore, working with scaling questions, and the "Osborn Checklist," a creativity technique created by Alex Osborn.

Structuring coaching talks with the TO-GROW model

As awkwardly as Egon Pilcher may have handled the coffee machine – his use of coaching questions was skillful. Instead of simply going ahead and asking, he followed a clear structure. John Whitmore's GROW model (see text box) offers a useful sequence of questions. A structure like this helps to achieve results for a distinct, well-bounded subject within a given time frame. As such, it is appropriate for longer conversations, for which you take sufficient time and create an appropriate setting. As a general rule, a coaching talk based on the GROW model takes a minimum of 30 minutes. You don't want to use it for short interventions. I recommend the model – which I have slightly adapted into a very hands-on version – based on 20 years of experience. I call my version the TO-GROW model: TO stands for "topic" because the model is about finding a tangible solution for a very specific subject. GROW, in line with Whitmore's model, stands for "goals", "reality", the "options" you have, and the "will" to do it.

> **TO-GROW: An expedient conversation structure for individual topics**
>
> If you have the time to have a complete conversation with one of your staff members to help him or her identify a solution for a distinct topic (**TO = Topic**), you might find it helpful to follow the TO-GROW structure – based on John Whitmore's

GROW model. In a total of four sequences, you ask the following open questions:

1. **G = Goals:** The first step is to identify goals. Here, we need to distinguish between the subject-related goal ("what do we need a solution for?") and the goal of the talk ("what should we have achieved by the end of this conversation?"). Both need to be clarified.
   Typical G questions are these: *What is the goal of this conversation? What is a longer-term goal? What is a short-term goal? What are possible milestones? What can we use to measure success? What experiences can help you achieve this goal?*
2. **R = Reality:** This is about grasping the reality of the given situation. You ask about the current distance to the goal, about attitudes, processes, and structures.
   Typical R questions are: *What is happening at the moment? What is the conclusion? What is your capacity situation? Who else is involved? What works and what doesn't? What is missing? What keeps you from doing this? What can motivate you? How often have you tried to find a solution?*
3. **O = Options:** This sequence of questions deals with the different options you have. It is best to look at the big picture first, then break it down into its details.
   Typical O questions are these: *What are the two main options? What else could you do? What advantages and disadvantages do these options have? If money were "no object," what would you do? What could work? What could you start with?*
4. **W = Will:** The last set of questions deals with the strong will to achieve a goal on a path that has shown to be realistic, and to stay on the ball. ("Who wants to do what by when, and how can I ensure that success will be sustainable?")
   Typical W questions are these: *What will you do now? What option do you choose? What will you start with? What could stop you, and what would you do then? Who else should be involved? What further support would be good to have?*

This is how a conversation with a TO-GROW structure proceeds

For the story about Egon and Karl, the TO-GROW structure was cut a bit shorter. Let's look at what Egon is doing here. He begins by suggesting to Karl that they discuss a very distinct and specific problem: The unsatisfactory coffee supply. He also makes an effort to create a good setting. With Karl's consent, both men move to a coffee corner. Egon asks Karl about his goals. Karl doesn't want that kind of stress anymore; he also says he wants all employees to be able to get coffee from the machine any time they like. The first goal can be achieved during the conversation itself: By having a plan, which helps Karl to calm down. To actually improve the coffee situation, he will need to take certain steps after the conversation.

Next, Egon performs a reality check and asks about the current coffee situation. It turns out that everyone – grouped by the "hallways" in the company – indulges in their individual preferences. They've told Karl that they will get their own coffee, but they keep forgetting about it – then they come complaining to Karl. He, in turn, is fed up with that. He says: We've tried this, and it doesn't work. Next, Egon asks about options. Karl instantly remembers there are coffee vendors that provide office service. But it might not be wise to rely on one vendor only, he says. Finally, Egon asks Karl what he's going to do. This is the point where Karl gets back into his role as responsible manager. The fact he had gotten out of that role had caused his anger. At this point, he says: I am the person in charge, so I'll make a decision. I'll notify the office occupants of my decision to find a new solution for keeping the coffee machines filled, and ask for their suggestions. In other words, he's reclaimed control of the situation, which stops him from feeling as if he is everyone's doormat.

In a real, extensive coaching talk, you will probably take more time for each of the four GROW steps. For instance, in a reality check you may want to go on to explore the "dark corners" using the flashlight method, and thus bring issues to the surface that are not immediately obvious. One question could be: "Who benefits most if nothing changes?" The same is true for options: For more demanding problems, you take more time. As a general rule, there should be at least two options; it may be helpful to think through as many as five. What's even more important, however, is how you start such a conversation – so let's go back to the start. It is important to always ensure clarity on what the topic is, and what you can and want to achieve in the course of your session. The risk you want to avoid is diving into the subject too fast. Also, remember there's a topic-related goal and a goal for the session as such. So, ask questions such as "What, exactly, do you want to achieve within the next 30 minutes?" A possible reply could be: "Some feedback would be great." Or: "I would love to get three new ideas." In short, be sure to establish a clear goal, so there will be no disappointment at the end.

And yes, it is completely okay to cover only parts of the TO-GROW model in your conversations or focus on individual elements. Sometimes, conversations end with a set of options; sometimes the goal is to set up an action plan or even simply to identify a goal. The key is to keep the TO-GROW structure in the back of your mind, so it can help you steer conversations effectively.

Economies of scale

"In your firm, it seems like the right hand doesn't know what the left hand's doing." This feedback from the city clerk had been a blow. Initially Danuta hadn't even found a slot in her schedule to accommodate the chamber of commerce's annual reception. Then an appointment had been shifted, and she'd made it to the event – only to run into one of her key customers, who immediately started complaining to her. Danuta's leasing firm handled the entire fleet management for her home town. As general manager, she knew only too well that things weren't running smoothly at the moment. But the way this man put it to her – throwing it in her face at a reception, and in this tone! – annoyed her so much she had to bite her tongue to avoid saying something she would instantly regret. She was relieved that she had to leave quickly to pick up her son from school. Her husband Eric was in Dubai, her housekeeper down with the flu. As a matter of fact, it was time she left. Danuta hurried across the visitors' parking lot, climbed into her high-powered black SUV, and drove off, the engine roaring.

The worst thing about this mess, Danuta thought as she was passing the shopping center and turning the corner to her son's school, is that there's always some truth even in the rudest complaint. The interface between their sales force and back office was, well …, a "work in progress" at best. The broadside from the city clerk was not the first feedback she'd received from customers on that subject. She had wanted to do something about it for the longest, only she never found the time. She urgently needed to talk to the heads of sales and back office but kept postponing the matter from week to week. To be very honest, she also lacked a good idea for a discussion starter.

As Danuta was approaching the school building, she saw her twelve-year-old son Ian standing on the sidewalk, waiting. The boy next to him looked like it could be his friend Robin, who lived one block away.

"Can Robin come with us?" Ian shouted excitedly, after he had ripped open the rear right-hand car door.

"Sure. Get in, you two superheroes," Danuta replied.

The first two miles, the car was quiet. Both boys were staring at their smartphones. Then, Ian seemed to have found a funny website.

"On a scale from one to ten, how much do you like discussing things? – Can I say eleven? – No! – Why not?" Ian read with a high-pitched, cracking voice.

"On a scale from one to ten, how forgetful are you? – One to what? – Ten. – What was your question? – Forget it. – What?" Robin, who had instantly googled the website on his smartphone, shouted at the same volume.

"On a scale from one to ten, how curious are you? – Can I see the scale?" Ian tried to outdo his friend.

Oh no, Danuta thought. The conference call with Ms. Rapps is supposed to start in five minutes – and here I have two twelve-year-olds in my backseat being silly. That's the last thing I need: That they keep reading these stupid jokes to each other. "Ian and Robin, could you please be quiet for a few minutes, so I can make a phone call?" she said, looking in the rear-view mirror. "After that, you can go back to googling your jokes. Okay?" That only seemed to set off the boys even more.

"On a scale from one to ten," Ian screamed, "how jealous are you? – Scale? Who's that and where does she live?" Ian and Robin both howled with laughter and could hardly contain themselves.

Danuta pushed the button on her steering wheel to start the phone. What else could she do? Then she hesitated and thought for a moment.

"Hey, you guys," she said – knowing that neither of them was listening, "You are so getting on my nerves! But you've just given me an idea, too …"

No joke: Using scaling questions in a coaching talk

Perhaps you've seen the Hollywood comedy *10* starring Bo Derek? George, the protagonist, suddenly meets the woman of his dreams – but she's on her way to the altar. His psychologist asks him where he would place her on a scale from one to ten. Hence the title of the movie. The psychologist fails to "scale down" George's obsession, which results in ever crazier entanglements. In the infinite expanses of questioning techniques, we sometimes find the most exotic-yet-useful plants flourishing in nooks and crannies right in front of us. The scaling question is one of them. Using a "scale from one to ten," it is possible to shape coaching talks in both an original and useful manner. You ask your counterpart to assess his or her emotional state or perception of a given situation on a scale from one to ten. Ten meaning close to orgiastic, one meaning almost dead. After a first spontaneous assessment, you can then continue to work with this scale.

When you apply scaling questions in people development, the goal is always to assess the status quo and then to ask whether it was better or worse before and what it takes to move up the scale. At the end of the day, it's all about resources. If the status used to be higher on the scale, what helped improve it? To improve it, what might help? In addition, the scale helps staff members focus on small steps instead of trying to start a revolution the next day. If, for instance, you ask, "What could you do to improve the situation by one point on the scale?" the focus will automatically be on smaller steps towards the solution. Some people like to use visualization in scaling. You may want to do that, but you don't have to. It is far more important to solve the resource issue.

This is how the "scale from one to ten" works in your talks with employees

Scaling questions are a useful technique when it comes to addressing long-standing structural conflict in a series of talks. Danuta's leasing firm is facing such a problem. Collaboration between the sales force and the back-office hasn't worked out for quite some time. Customers' feedback indicates that the left hand doesn't seem to know what the right hand does. Danuta intends to have a discussion to clear the air but has been putting it off for months. Her son Ian and his friend Robin then remind her she can try scaling questions, a technique she's familiar with. The key now is for Danuta to invite the head of sales and the head of the back-office to separate talks. Asking both for a joint assessment of their collaboration on a scale from one to ten would not get them anywhere. Danuta begins with the head of field sales: "On a scale from one to ten, how would you assess your collaboration with the back-office?" The answer comes instantly: The head of field sales replies, "four!" Next, she asks: "What is it like to be on four?" This is a reality check. The head of field sales describes the situation from his perspective. As a next step, Danuta asks whether the situation was better or worse before. Her colleague tells her they used to be a seven or eight just two years ago, when his back-office colleague was still motivated. Three months ago, he would have answered "0.5."

Well, if that's the case, it seems like things are moving here. Time for Danuta to address the resource question. Back when things were better, what were key factors contributing to that? When her colleague points them out, Danuta asks another, decisive question: "What does it take to get from four to five, so that our customers will notice, too?" The head of field sales now makes suggestions on what he will change and commits himself to implementing them. Danuta agrees to meet with him again in four weeks. Then she has the same conversation with the head of the back-office, again using a scale from one to ten. After both talks, she asks staff in field sales and the back-office to work together to identify solutions that will help them move one point forward on their respective scales. This keeps Danuta out of the process of developing a solution. She does stay a while longer, though, to facilitate the discussion and watch what's happening. Afterwards, she meets with both managers every few months to ask them the same question: "On a scale from one to ten ...?"

This goes on until there are clear improvements that are noticed and confirmed by customers.

Resourceful humans

"The couple I worked with this afternoon were really cute," Susanne told Nico. She was happy she'd been able to help Sandra in her session. She was also happy to see the young banker get such great support from her boyfriend, Ivan. After a long day at her office, Susanne was now hanging out with Nico, her partner, in their tastefully decorated apartment, which was located in a beautiful turn-of-the-century building in the center of Hamburg. Nico, who worked as an online editor for a renowned magazine publisher, had brought some of his work home, as he often did. He was lying on the bed, propped up against a large pillow, and typing on his notebook. Susanne was sitting cross-legged beside him, her iPad in her lap, chatting with a friend in Shanghai on the messenger app. At the same time, she was telling Nico about Sandra and Ivan. She avoided mentioning names or confidential details. In the background, a Spotify playlist was playing.

"Why don't you have a look at this e-mail I'm writing to HR," Nico interrupted her.

Susanne looked up from her tablet and looked at him. She didn't really like that tone of his. What was he doing?

Nico shoved his notebook towards her. "Just so you've seen it before I send it off," he added.

Susanne quickly scanned his draft, which was addressed to the firm's head of HR, and instantly found the crucial sentence: *Since I assume your silence to mean approval, I herewith accept the position as head of the online editorial team of our new publication* Vega Grill.

Resourceful humans

Susanne snapped the notebook shut, put it down between them, and asked, "You want to tell me what's happening here?"

"You know I sent them an internal application. As the head of the online team for our new special-interest magazine for vegan barbecuing. It's made it through the test phase and is going to market soon."

"So …?"

"Well, you can guess the rest. It's the same as always: Everything's long since been decided, like who will be what. They publish these vacancies as a formality because they have to. And, stupid me, I actually applied. Of course, I never got a reply. Nothing. Nada. Not even a confirmation of receipt from HR."

"I see. And so you're planning to send this sarky message to the head of HR at your publishing house. And you wanted me to read it before you send it off. Why's that?"

"No particular reason."

"Nico!"

"Alright, maybe I could find another way to deal with HR. You got a better idea?"

"Can I ask you three crazy questions?"

"Go ahead."

"What would be the funniest solution?"

"The funniest? I could … print out my application, get it framed, and FedEx it to HR."

"Not that funny, Nico."

"You're being judgmental!"

"I know. Let's take this a bit further. What kind of solution would give you a real thrill?"

"A thrill??"

"Yeah, like a kick."

"Well, our head of HR does have eyes ... I imagine a one-on-one talk could be an, errm, emotionally stimulating situation."

"Un-huh. Interesting ... Okay, last question: What would your father do, if he were in your shoes?"

"My dad ... oh yeah, of course you had to bring him up. He would probably clarify everything in his super-rational, conscientious, and super-Nordic manner, always true to form."

"Well, at least we've got a few alternative solutions now. You can send off the mail as it is. You can resolve the issue in a funny way, or in a thrilling way, or the way your father would. You've got a preference?"

"I guess I'll go for thrills plus father."

Sometimes, slightly crazy questions help untie the knot

Some conversation situations can be really tricky. People want help, then again they don't. Just like Nico. He wants his girlfriend to "have a quick look at" the sarcastic e-mail he has written to his HR boss, and which would do nothing for him in the firm. Being a coach, Susanne instantly realizes that this is a hidden call for help. Almost like saying, "go away to me." Nico supposedly doesn't want anything – but in truth, he wants everything. When people send such contradictory signals, they are under stress. They are fixated on one solution, which they have already laid out for themselves. Remember Barry Oshry's doors number one and two? In a situation like this, people are fixated on one door and can't even imagine there are any other doors somewhere in this world. But their subconscious is in rebellion. In this setting, someone knows more than they think they know. There is always more than one solution.

Lateral thinking can achieve a lot in a paradoxical situation like this. When you ask out-of-the-box questions, solution energy emerges. As soon as your counterpart begins to look at the problem from a new, perhaps surprising perspective, the knot will come undone. So, after making a reality check to know what's going on, don't hesitate to ask seemingly absurd questions: What would be the most stupid, the most boring, the most naive, the most daring solution? What would your best friend do? Or your arch-rival? How would your mom go about it? Your dad? What would a four-year-old do? This approach – using playful, experimental questions – taps into the big toolbox of creativity techniques. It is based, above all, on the well-known Osborn list. Concepts that help creativity are sometimes helpful in coaching, too.

> **Osborn's checklist: Learning from the pioneer of creative thinking**
>
> Alex F. Osborn (1888–1966) was an advertising executive. Today, he is considered the pioneer of creative thinking. One of the key concepts he created is creative problem-solving.
>
> Around 1957, Osborn developed a list of questions for idea generation, which is now known as the Osborn list or checklist. With different sets of questions, an idea or existing product is considered from different angles.
>
> Among other things, this list includes "replacing," "reversing," or "combining" as possible approaches. Related questions could be: Different material? Turn the item upside down? Mix products? According to the Osborn list, the invention of the iPhone, as the first smartphone ever, is a *combination* of existing products and technologies: the mobile phone, the computer, the mp3 player, the touchscreen, etc.

A word of caution is in order here: If you want to use crazy questions in coaching, some prerequisites have to be in place. It's a bit like the fireworks on New Year's Eve: While they are basically harmless, you should be able to handle them. First off, you need a lot of self-assuredness to confront someone with lateral-thinking questions. If you're afraid of a role conflict, and you fear you might make a fool of yourself as a manager, forget about asking absurd questions.

Let's assume you're not afraid. It is important to make sure that you're in a good energetic condition. Lateral thinking is a playful and creative approach, and it doesn't work when you're stressed. Also, make sure to create a setting that promotes a trustful atmosphere. I presume your conversation won't take place on a bed – as it does in our example – but you may want to keep this image in the back of your mind, as a symbol of the extra amount of trust that this technique requires.

Last key point: Announce what you are going to do! With the words, "Do you mind if I ask you three crazy questions?" Susanne requests an okay from her partner. Then, she asks him questions he would have never thought of himself. What would be the funniest solution? What kind of solution would give him a thrill or adrenaline kick? How would his father go about this? Nico finally chooses a combination of "thrilling" and "father". What could this mean?

Nico could request a talk with his boss, look her deeply in the eyes, and try to charm her. That (or what happens next) is the thrilling part. At the same time, he could seek to clarify things – that is, ask how his application is coming along, and why he hasn't gotten any feedback. That is the "father" part. Is it really true that there was some behind-the-scenes fiddling, or is that just some story he made up in his mind? If there is a grain of truth to it, the HR boss might not openly admit it. But at least Nico would give her a chance to explain her perspective on things. He would stop jumping to conclusions and would not make himself vulnerable by sending an inappropriately sarcastic e-mail.

Chapter 9: Takeaways

- When you use coaching conversations, key factors are your attitude, a trust-based framework, and moving the slider between Push and Pull. There are lots of questioning techniques; most of them work.
- If you have time for a long conversation, it may be helpful to use a structured approach. The TO-GROW model entails questions on four topics: goals, reality, options, and will.
- With coaching talks, there is always both a topic-related goal and a session-related goal. Don't leap into the subject too abruptly. It's better to begin by clarifying what the outcome of a (longer) conversation should be.
- If someone is stuck in a structural conflict, scaling questions ("on a scale from one to ten") can help mobilize resources and focus on small, feasible steps. "What could you do to improve the status quo from 5 to 6?"
- Crazy, lateral-thinking questions are helpful when someone is stuck. They bring creativity into the game and open new perspectives. Proceed with caution, however, when using questions of this type. It is critical to ask such questions only in a particularly trustful setting.

Chapter 10
Problem-solving in all directions – or:
Back to the future

Problem-solving often fails because people only think in one of three possible directions: Either they are focused on the past and unable to disengage themselves from the blame question, at least in their perception. Or they stick to the present, analyzing the problem to death and forgetting to develop a vision for the future. Or they immediately leap into the solution because they think there's no need to analyze the problem and acknowledge the past. An agile problem-solving process considers three perspectives – past, present, and future – dynamically, considering each of them as thoroughly as the situation requires. The focus is on the desirable future state.

An overcast day in Berlin. Leo is hurrying to his boss's office. It's the third boss in five years. Leo is upset. As the business editor in charge at a private TV news network, he has an opportunity to meet Han H. Hirshberg, the US business guru, for an interview. The only problem is, he'll have to fly to Hawaii to meet him. Everyone knows Hirshberg is never available for interviews, so this is a unique opportunity. Now this: His flight to Hawaii has not been approved. "What do these people think?", he wonders, "that I want to spend 22 hours on a plane just for fun? ... or to see Hula girls?" Leo is furious. That's why he's running. From the editorial office in Dorotheenstrasse, he cuts across downtown Berlin to get to the network's administrative center. Past the Dussmann department store, past several dusty construction sites, past crowds of Chinese tourists fiddling with their selfie sticks. He reaches the office building, storms through the entrance door, runs up the stairs to the second floor, and directly into the office of Otto Hartmann, the CEO. The boss's secretary never even has a chance to stop him.

"It can't go on like this," Leo firmly says, after he's calmed down somewhat. He is sitting in the conference corner, having a coffee with the network's CEO. "I need to be able to do my work. Which occasionally includes making long trips. That interview with Hirshberg is going to be a hit! It will get us lots of clicks from top decision-makers, both in our media library and on YouTube."

"Have you had similar problems in the past with similar trips?" the CEO wants to know.

"What do you mean, similar trips?"

"Well – trips that have pleasant aspects, along with the business purpose. After all, you're going to fly to a dream destination. I can imagine there've been other colleagues before who arranged their interview trips so as to enjoy some of the touristic highlights."

"I'm not going to Hawaii for fun."

"Of course not. But the colleague that refused to approve the trip might have had a reason. Looking at your travels over the past few months, is there an increased number of touristic destinations?"

"No, definitely not."

"And how about the other editors? It's our administrative clerks' job to monitor resource efficiency. Perhaps someone or something has raised their suspicions before, so they react that way when they read 'Hawaii'."

"What do I care?! Fact is, I'm not going on vacation, I want to seize a unique opportunity to get an interview with Hirshberg. Everyone knows he refuses talk to the US media."

"That may be true. On the other hand, in my years at several TV networks, I've seen cases where editors thought they really needed to meet people in the Caribbean, then it turned out these same people came to Frankfurt a few weeks later so they could have met them at the hotel ..."

"You know what?" Leo interrupts him, rising from his seat. "Forget it. Thanks for your time. I'm not interviewing Hirshberg; I'll get busy with something else instead."

When a one-sided focus on the past gets in the way of a good solution

"Happy families are all alike; every unhappy family is unhappy in its own way," goes the famous first sentence of Leo Tolstoy's 1878 novel *Anna Karenina*. A very common reason why families make themselves unhappy is that they keep fixated on the past. Discussions in these families tend to center around who is to blame for what. When a problem emerges, the key question is not, "What happened?" or, "What could be a possible solution?" but: "*Why* has this happened?" For instance, someone might say, "Why didn't you empty the dishwasher?" Which is irrelevant when it comes to clarifying *who* will empty the dishwasher *when*. But systems that keep focused on the past are primarily interested in the question of guilt. They also find it hard to forget things. "You've done it again" or "How often have I told you that ..." are popular phrases here. Have you experienced similar things at work? People from families like these – or with similar experiences from other social contexts – have an inner automatic reflex that, as soon as problems emerge, immediately causes them to ask the Why and Whose Fault questions – hence their predictable response to problems or conflicts at work. Dealing with the present and developing a vision for a possible solution require reflection and deliberate communication.

The past needs to be acknowledged – but it's not a safe place to go

We humans like to deal with the past because we believe our memory to be reliable. The truth is, every perception of reality is fragile and full of deceptions and contradictions – but that is something we like to push aside. When we talk about the past, we believe we are safe. Past events are facts to us. Again, these are appearances. "The past is a gentle goddess," as Goethe put it. As many other things, our concept of the past is a mental construct that permanently changes. Perhaps you've experienced this before: You seem to have a very clear memory of a certain place. Then you see an old photograph of that same place, and you realize it looks different from how you had remembered it. Your memory has changed over time. So, should we forget about the past altogether? Definitely not. Everything we experience leaves emotional traces. Our past may not be a safe place, but we care about it. We want it acknowledged. That is what CEO Hartmann could have done: Briefly acknowledge the anger and frustration Leo feels because his request has been denied. After that, he should have stopped talking about why this happened or why it still happens. The question about who's to blame doesn't do much in the way of problem-solving.

Second try

An overcast day in Berlin. Leo is hurrying to his boss's office. She's the fourth person in six years to be in the CEO's seat. Leo is upset. He wants to go to Dubai to meet Adriano, the Milan-based king of fine furniture, for an interview. Leo initiated this contact a while ago. For the first time, Adriano is willing to give a journalist insights into his secretive empire. Now this: Administration has not approved his trip to Dubai! Leo is furious. That's why he is running. From the editorial office, he cuts

Second try

through downtown Berlin to his company's administrative center. He runs past the Borchardt restaurant, past white horse carriages, past young men sitting on benches with beer bottles. When he reaches the office building, he storms through the entrance door, runs up the stairs to the second floor, and directly into the office of Eva Herberger, the CEO. The boss's assistant never has a chance to stop him.

"It can't go on like this," Leo says after he's calmed down somewhat. He's sitting in a visitor's chair opposite the CEO's desk. "I had the same hassle before, under the last CEO. Now it's the same thing again: I'm on to a big story, and I'm being stonewalled by administration. Can you imagine: This is the very first time Adriano Minetti is willing to talk to a journalist about his empire – and he's chosen me! I really need to go to Dubai. Right now."

"Okay, what exactly is the problem?"

"I got an e-mail saying my trip hasn't been approved."

"I understand. And the sender was the clerk in charge?"

"Yes, of course"

"And he was referring to the same trip? There's no way he might have confused something?"

"Absolutely not."

"The clerk had received your complete request?"

"Yes, he did. As always. My request was even attached to that mail."

"In that case, I don't understand why your request was denied."

"I don't either. That's why I'm here."

"Could it be that several colleagues have requested expensive trips?"

"I don't have a clue, and I don't care anyway. Oh my god, after all this time I've managed to get this close to Adriano!"

"And you can't meet this gentleman in Italy, where his company is based?"

"Well, this isn't an audience with the Pope. Adriano is constantly on the move. When he tells me he's going to have time to see me in Dubai, I have to seize the opportunity."

"Have you thought about using Skype?"

"You know what?" Leo interrupts her, rising from his seat. "Forget it. Thanks for your time. Let Adriano tell his success story to another magazine. I'll get working on something else."

If you try to solve problems focusing on the present only, you'll go around in circles.

I suppose you've seen the Hollywood comedy *Groundhog Day* starring Bill Murray. Everyone has. Murray plays a TV weatherman who is caught in a time loop and relives the same day again and again. There are lots of families where the same problems and conflicts are caught in a continuous loop. The same issues are discussed over and over, the families never learn from their conflicts. They keep fighting and making up again – and shortly afterwards, fighting about the same thing again. Their solution approach resembles the *Groundhog Day* plot. That's why families like these only appear to be better, at first glance, than those forever stuck in the past and looking for culprits. Sure, it's good to consider problems thoroughly and to discuss conflicts. But when this fails to produce learning effects, these systems are just another version of Tolstoy's unhappy family. Just like Sisyphus, the character from Greek mythology, people keep rolling the same rock up the hill, until the rock rolls back down, and everything starts again. People who've been socialized like that tend to bury themselves in problems at work, too, without finding sustainable solutions.

Problem-solving requires a vision of the target state

Looking at a problem closely at first, without immediately thinking about solutions, is basically a good approach. You need clarity on what the matter is in order to find a fitting solution. In the case of complex and protracted conflicts, it may be necessary to shine a light into all the dark corners and look at everything you might not have noticed at first glance. It is also important to rule out misunderstandings. Another thing that can't hurt is a dose of healthy skepticism – and checking back whether things really are as your coachee has described them. In that sense, Leo's CEO is right to ask all those questions. But there is a point where she oversteps the mark, which causes Leo to get up and leave. If you don't have a particular reason, it doesn't make much sense to question even the most obvious facts. So, if you want effectiveness, resist the temptation to ask too many details. Also, penetrating questions such as "Have you tried this?" or "Have you considered that?" can quickly destroy your rapport with a staff member who is frustrated and looking for solutions. The key is to not get lost in analysis, and to set the course towards a solution early on. In due time, you need what Steve de Shazer and others have called the "solution vision": A tangible image of the desired future state.

Third try

An overcast day in Berlin. Leo is hurrying to his boss's office. It's the fifth CEO in seven years. Leo is upset. Sarah Bangs, the newly appointed CEO of one of the largest pharmaceutical companies worldwide, has invited selected journalists to accompany her on a camera safari in Kenya. In the course of that trip, she intends to tell them about the opportunities for the pharmaceutical industry that exist in threshold markets. Not surprising, Leo thinks, that his flight to Africa was not approved. The key word here is "safari." Leo is foaming with rage, which is why he's running. He cuts across downtown Berlin to get to his company's administrative center – past the Lafayette Galleries, past waiting taxi cabs, past a group of Bavarian retirees about to climb off their tourist coach. He reaches the office building, storms through the entrance door, runs up the stairs to the second floor, and directly into the office of Paul Britt, the CEO. The boss's assistant never has a chance to stop him.

"It can't go on like this," Leo firmly states, after he has calmed down somewhat. He is standing at the window with his boss, looking down at the large square below. "It should be clear to everybody that I'm not going on this safari just for fun. Sarah Bangs is one of the most exciting female top executives worldwide. Her pharma company is the first to make real money in Africa. I want to find out how she did it."

"What kind of format were you thinking of to present your findings?"

"I don't know yet. First, I have to get there and see Ms. Bangs in person. But they don't let me."

"How would you like this solved?"

"That's simple: I want to get this trip approved. Like I've been telling you."

"Well, I don't think that'll be enough to convince the clerk in charge. It would be the wrong signal. What else could you do?"

"I don't know. I've got no clue. I thought you could help me."

"Alright. I suppose we'll have to establish clearer rules for cases like this. You want to put together some suggestions?"

"That won't help to solve my current problem."

"I know, but next time you would know better what to expect."

"You know what?" Leo interrupts her, walks to the door, and turns as he says: "Forget it. Thanks for your time."

Thinking of the future only is not always healthy ...

Futurism was the name of an art movement around 1910, which was out to establish a completely new culture. Filippo Marinetti published the *Futurist Manifesto*. You haven't heard of this manifesto, nor can you spontaneously think of a famous Futurist painter? And you aren't under the impression that we've been living in a new culture since 1910? Small wonder – making the future is not that easy. "A future always needs a past," as the philosopher Odo Marquard so succinctly put it. If you simply start fantasizing about what the future could look like, it is likely the actual future will be very different from what you've imagined. "We want a better life for our children." This is a statement often heard in future-oriented families. Well, they may be in for a shock when that future materializes. Children often do what *they* think is right – not what their parents thought of as "better." Also, parents miss out on their own lives if they only live for their kids' future. People with a strong future bias think about the "What for?" question all the time. Typical phrases are: "What am I am standing here for, discussing this with you?" Or: "What do you think you'll get out of this?" Or: "Why do you think I'm doing this to myself?" This, too, can be a road to hell: if you don't acknowledge past developments, nor look at what is happening right here and now.

Solutions are in the future – but there's a path leading there

No question: The solution to a problem is always in the future. It is all about a desired future state – as opposed to the present state, which is problematic. But there is always a path that leads into the future; on this path, both the past and the present play a role. Some people think coaching is about immediately pushing for a solution. CEO Britt practices an extreme form of this. She is not interested in dealing with the past and present. Her first question is: How can we prevent this in the future? By acting this way, she demonstrates to Leo that she doesn't really care about his current problem. It can be quite an ignorant way to act. Leo wants to be understood and acknowledged first. He needs a solution for his current problem. Only the last step can and should be about how things can be improved in the future. Yes: A vision for how to solve both the current problem and all similar future problems would be ideal. So, please don't go at it like the bull at a gate!

Fourth try – bingo!

A sunny day in Berlin. Leo is hurrying to his boss's office. It's his sixth boss in eight years. Leo is upset. He is working on a spectacular story about organized crime in European agriculture. At long last, Henk – the former head of European operations at an agricultural group, is willing to talk. But only one-on-one. No e-mails, no telephone, no Skype. The problem is: Henk has retired to the Dutch Antilles – and Leo's company has denied his travel request. "Research on European agriculture in the Caribbean?" one of the clerks has written in his e-mail. Outrageous, Leo thinks. He is so mad he is running. He cuts across downtown Berlin to get to his company's administrative center, passing groups of people who are laughing and enjoying the summer day. Leo gets to the office building, storms through the entrance door, and runs up the stairs to the second floor. The CEO doesn't have a personal assistant anymore. There are assistant teams now, each of them assigned to several executives. The CEO, Sophia Hellmeyer, has visitors. Her office door is open. Sophia steps outside for a moment to tell Leo she's still busy but will meet him in about 20 minutes. She suggests meeting at the coffee shop across the street.

"You seemed very upset up there," Sophia says after she's picked up a coffee and a cappuccino at the bar and sat down with Leo at a small table. "Tell me what's going on."

"I am constantly accused of going on business trips for fun. Every time it's an exotic destination, my travel requests are denied. It's been like this for years, and none of the other CEOs has ever helped me. Hartmann was only interested in who's to blame. Herberger was better, at least she looked at the problem. But she didn't have a solution. Britt was the worst: Never tried to help me, just asked me to suggest new regulations."

"Well, I can't comment on my predecessors. I'm sure you understand that. But you're one of our best on the editorial staff, and I don't want you to have problems with our administrative staff. We are here to facilitate and support your work. Also, you are absolutely right when you expect us to show some understanding for your work. Of course, we all know that journalists don't travel for fun. I'm sorry if you gained another impression."

"It's okay. In every other aspect, the network is a great employer."

"What could be the problem with this latest request?"

"The clerk working on it wrote something about doing research in the Caribbean on a subject like European agriculture."

"Do you get her point?"

"Well, to be honest I didn't go into a lot of detail in my request."

"What might make it easier for that clerk to make a favorable decision?"

"I could explain things better. My contact won't be in Europe for quite a while, and he insists on a one-on-one appointment. I hadn't mentioned that."

"Look. I really don't want to interfere. That's not my idea of leadership. But you are free to tell that clerk that you talked to me."

"And that I realized that in my request I hadn't explained the reasons properly?"

"Sure."

"And so I'll give them the reasons now?"

"That might work. If it doesn't, we can talk again."

"Great, thanks."

"One more thing. In your opinion, does it even make sense to have every single travel request reviewed? Seeing as there've never been any fun trips or other misconduct?"

"Well, we do have colleagues – I won't say who it is – who've actually gone to the Caribbean or the Gulf or other destinations without doing lots of research there …"

"How can you make sure you won't be lumped in with them in the future?"

"Well … I could add more details to my requests from the start, like the reasons why I need to make that trip."

"That might work, don't you think? I know it will be more work for you. But then again, as a journalist, you shouldn't have a problem writing a few good statements …"

"You've got a point there," Leo says, grinning, and finishes his coffee. While Sophia gets up, he looks out the window and lets his gaze wonder across the heads of all the people that are sitting in the sun and enjoying their coffee. That broad-shouldered man there with the baseball hat, sitting all alone at that table in the back … could that be … no, impossible … yeah, of course it was him … Han H. Hirshberg!! What was he doing in Berlin?

Problem-solving in three directions: past, present, and future

Finally, Leo feels he has rapport with his boss! In her conversation with him, Sophia does several good things: She ensures an atmosphere of trust. And since she doesn't have time for him right away, she suggests meeting at the coffee bar in twenty minutes. In their conversation, she gives Leo the opportunity to vent his frustration about his recurring problem and the fact that nobody's been able to solve it so far. She listens calmly and signals her understanding. She expresses regret about the unfortunate state of things. As the executive in charge of administration, she assures Leo that the administrative staff are supposed to support the editorial team. During all this time, Sophia avoids judging what has happened in the past. She doesn't adopt Leo's perspective or blame the clerks. She communicates with empathy and indicates she's aware of Leo's frustration – which is sufficient to acknowledge past events. Then, she steers Leo's attention to the present. Asking a series of skillful questions, she gets him to recognize the motives of the clerk who had denied his request. In a sense, she builds a bridge from the past to the present. And, indeed, there is a blind spot: Leo hasn't made much of an effort to add some background information to his travel request. Through her questions, Sophia makes Leo realize this and identify a solution: He could send the clerk a more detailed explanation of why he needs to make his trip. With that, Sophia also builds a bridge to the future. How about if Leo put more effort into specifying the reasons for his business trips to exotic destinations?

> **Having solution-oriented coaching conversations**
>
> If you look for sustainable solutions, don't charge ahead to the future right away. Begin by "flying a loop" over the past and present – making it as long as necessary and as short as possible. Then step on it and take off towards the future (Figure 10.1).

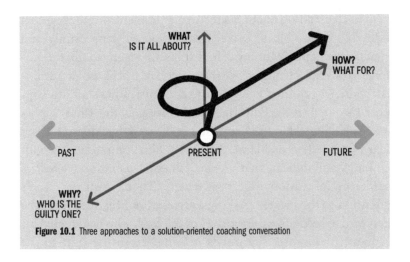

Figure 10.1 Three approaches to a solution-oriented coaching conversation

Acknowledge what is happening, value what happened, then look ahead

In principle, there are three ways to approach a problem. The first is past-oriented. Why are things the way they are? This question can make sense, but it can easily lead into fruitless discussions on who is to blame for a situation. The second approach focuses on the present: What exactly is the problem? This is about sober analysis. The risk, however, is to get lost in the problem rather than come up with a solution. The third approach is future-oriented: What are we doing this for? And what could be a possible solution? This is certainly the crucial question. But if you come straight to the point, it's unlikely you will really engage the other person. A meaningful combination of all three approaches is illustrated in Figure 10.1: Acknowledge the present, fly a brief loop over the past to acknowledge it, too – then zoom ahead into the future. With your analysis of the past and present, you should take as much time as needed and as little time as possible. How much that will be in each case depends on the problem. Conflicts that have been smoldering for a while obviously call for a longer glance at the past – after all, even the past can be a resource. So it's best to leave all your options open. At the end of the day, what matters is the solution envisaged and the pull energy that will carry you to your goal. Root-cause analysis is important but, as a technique, it should also help to release solution energy.

All of this applies to conversations with employees – and, who knows, it might even apply to every problem of humankind.

Chapter 10: Takeaways

- The past should always be acknowledged. If a problem is approached solely with a focus on the past, however, all discussions and considerations will revolve around the "Why?" and get bogged down in recurring questions about guilt and blame.
- Getting to the present, it is important to acknowledge what *is*. However, if you spend too much time analyzing a problem, you risk missing the point at which it would be important to develop a vision for the solution.
- The solution to a problem is always in the future, as it is supposed to lead to the desired future state of things. Still, it may be counter-productive to leap to future questions too quickly.
- For a sustainable solution to the problem, make sure to "fly a loop" over the past and present, before you gather momentum with a vision for your solution and plunge ahead into the future.
- In acknowledging the past and analyzing the present, make sure to be as brief as possible yet as comprehensive as needed. How much time you invest here depends on the nature of the problem.

Closing remarks

Now that you've reached the end of this book, I hope you feel both empowered and motivated to use coaching techniques in your management practice to increase your impact.

What else do I wish you? Above all, curiosity, a sense of humor, and serenity.

- Stay **curious**. Your people are likely to have more skills than you think.
- Stay **humorous**. Creative solutions often spring from humor.
- Stay **serene**. Business is important, but there are more important things in life.

Sincerely yours,
Masha Ibeschitz

Further reading

The following is a list of recommended further reading.

Bandura, Albert: *Social Learning Theory* (Prentice-Hall Series in Social Learning) Paperback – Facsimile 1976

Bannink, Fredrike: *1001 Solution-Focused Questions. Handbook for Solution-Focused Interviewing.* W. W. Norton & Company, 2010

Collignon, Gerard and Pascal Legrand: *Understand to Be Understood. By Using the Process Communication Model.* Xlibris, 2016

De Shazer, Steve: *More Than Miracles: The State of the Art of Solution-Focused Brief Therapy* (Haworth Brief Therapy), 2007

Goldsmith, Marshall: *What Got You Here Won't Get You There. How Successful People Become Even More Successful.* Profile Books, 2008

Hawkins, Peter: *Creating a Coaching Culture.* Open University Press, 2012

Hersey, Paul und Ken Blanchard: *Management of Organizational Behaviour.* Prentice Hall, 1982

Hofert, Svenja: *Agiler führen. Einfache Maßnahmen für bessere Teamarbeit, mehr Leistung und höhere Kreativität (Agile leadership. Simple steps to enhance teamwork, performance, and creativity).* SpringerGabler, 2016

Kahler, Taibi: *Prozesskommunikation: Der Schlüssel für konstruktive Kommunikation.* Process Training and Consulting, 2003

Maslow, Abraham; Frager, Robert: *Motivation and Personality*, Pearson, 1970

May, Charles and Jayne May: *Are You VUCA-Ready?* CreateSpace Independent Publishing, 2014

Meyer, Erin: *The Culture Map. Decoding How People Think, Lead, and Get Things Done Across Cultures.* PublicAffairs, 2014

Osborn, Alex: *Unlocking your creative power.* Hamilton Books, 2009

Oshry, Barry: *In the Middle.* Power & Systems Publishing, 1994

Oshry, Barry: *Seeing Systems. Unlocking the Mysteries of Organizational Life.* Berrett-Koehler Publishers, 2007

Sinek, Simon: *Why leaders eat last,* 2014

Wehrle, Martin: *Die 500 besten Coaching-Fragen. Das große Workbook für Einsteiger und Profis zur Entwicklung der eigenen Coaching-Fähigkeiten (The 500 best coaching questions. A big work book to help beginners and pros develop their coaching skills).* ManagerSeminare Verlag, 2016

Whitmore, John: *Coaching for Performance – A Practical Guide,* nb, 1996

Thanks!

Usually there's only one name on a book cover, sometimes two or three, but the truth is a bit different: Every book manuscript is the result of an extensive network of thoughts, ideas, stories, memories, quotes, emotions, and energies.

I want to thank the following people who have contributed to this book in one or several of the ways mentioned:

My clients. I am happy to be able to work with them and keep learning from them. Together we are on a journey of passion and creativeness. There are still so many resources waiting to be discovered!

My husband Rainer. I can always count on his love, support, and patience, and I greatly value his dry sense of humor. He is the epitome of humorous serenity.

My son Peter. At 5, he is at an ideal age to ask ingenuous questions. (My favorite one is: "Mom, what is above the universe?")

My parents and grandparents. As someone that grew up in a family of farmers and entrepreneurs, and who is aware of the importance of having strong roots, I was always encouraged by them to try out new things. They were living examples of how you achieve your goals with determination and initiative. They've also taught me to respect the universe, to treat other living beings and things with respect. Thanks to them, I've understood that success is a result of hard work, trust in yourself and others, and always a little bit of luck.

My coaches and mentors. They help me to keep reflecting and learning, and, above all, to implement things – in all areas of life and in a variety of cultures.

My life companions: Claudia, Georg, T.A., Renate, Alex, and my sister Eva. When the going gets tough, they are always there for me.

Dorothee Köhler and Jörg Achim Zoll. I had originally started by simply writing down my experiences and findings as anonymized stories. Nevertheless I realized that it would better serve the purposes and standards of this book if the sories were disguised. These two professionals helped me get it done. Working with them was a true pleasure.

My feedback providers. They have read the finished manuscript in confidence, and given me their honest, thoughtful, and constructive feedback. It has helped me adjust individual passages or express myself more precisely where necessary. Time and again, the impetus that comes from honest feedback is invaluable.

About the author

Photo: Uwe Klössing

Masha Ibeschitz knows the ropes in the executive world. As a reflection guide and executive coach with a degree in business management, she serves clients around the globe. She works with executives of global companies in different industries to enhance their impact in the VUCA world – beset by volatility, uncertainty, change, and ambiguity – and learn how to use coaching to minimize pressure, resolve conflicts, and develop their people into top performers. As a management trainer, she regularly hosts leadership journeys in different countries, which frequently includes teaching the basics of coaching to managers.

After graduating from university, Masha Ibeschitz set out to gather hands-on experience in several industries, managing projects and working in business development. Since starting her coaching practice in 1995, she has continually updated her knowledge and obtained a series of recognized qualifications. In 2014, she was the first and so far only woman in the German-speaking region to qualify as a Kirkpatrick® Partner. As such, she is authorized to issue the Kirkpatrick® Bronze Certification.

With more than 20 years of experience, Masha Ibeschitz is one of the top names on the coaching scene. She is also a partner at a global firm specializing in executive development. Masha regularly publishes articles in business magazines and online media. In 2016, she contributed to the acclaimed book by Ina Weinbauer Heidel, *What makes training really work. 12 levers of transfer effectiveness*.

Masha Ibeschitz lives in Vienna, Austria, with her family.

Index

A adapt   19
Ad-hoc support   67–68
advising   83
ambiguity   17–18
attention   114
attitude   22, 29, 39–40, 45
autonomy   60

B Bandura   99–100
beginner   82–83, 98–99
blame *see* guilt
Blanchard   99, 105
body language   118
brain fog   54–55

C capabilities   26, 48, 55, 67, 98, 100–101
cause-and-effect chain   137–138
Cautious Performer   95, 99–100, 105, 107
change   17, 19, 33, 45, 80
change of perspective   78
clarity   124, 147, 165
Clinton, Bill   34
coachability   95, 98–100, 107
coaching   28, 47, 82–83, 157, 167
– capabilities   98
– coachability   95, 108
– conditions   114
– definition   83
– different from mentoring and teaching   94
– experience   12
– impetus   93
– occasions   63
– questions   72
– role   77
– setting   109, 117, 124
– situations   98
– skills   11, 79
– solution-oriented conversations   171
– talk   117, 119, 144, 146, 149, 157, 171
– techniques   11, 44, 54, 61, 138, 141
– toolbox   31
– tools   40, 45, 67, 71, 78, 141
commitment   105
communication   31, 34–36, 51
– directive   82, 84
– non-directive   82–84
– patterns   44

– pull   84–85
– push   84
– stress-free   118
company Christmas party   47
company success
complexity   17–18
conditions
– predictable   21–22
confidentiality   117
conflict   54, 61
– facilitation   67–68, 77
– mediation   67–68
– moderation   77
– resolution   75, 157, 165
– structural   157
– surfacing   75
convictions   34, 123, 130, 139
corporate culture   37, 89, 92
creativity   67–68
cultural diversity   130

D day-to-day business   26, 44
delegating   25, 67, 100
de Shazer, Steve   165
development guide   11
development stages   99–101
development targets   66
– long-term   67
– short-term   67–68
digitalization   17, 80
disempowerment   22
Disillusioned Learner   100

E elevator principle   34–35, 37, 41, 44, 46
emotions   45, 100, 107, 119, 150
employee development   29, 34–36, 45, 65, 67, 78, 94, 133–134, 139, 150
energy   25, 45
– management   130
– solution energy   67–68, 173
Enthusiastic Beginner   100, 106
equal footing   83, 94
ethics   92

F feedback   66, 128, 156
flashlight method   147, 165
focus   112
future
– fixation on the   167
Futurism   167

G goals 28, 89, 92, 144–145, 157
Goethe, Johann Wolfgang von 162
GROW model 144–145
guilt
– focus on 161, 173

H Harmonizer (PCM) 34–36, 44, 55, 76, 105, 124
help, call for 154
Hersey, Paul 99, 105
high-potentials 65

I Idea generation 67–68
Imaginer (PCM) 34–36
impact 28, 44, 61
inner child 132, 133, 139
interjections 114, 119, 124
interpretations 108, 122
interventions 63, 68, 71, 144

K Kahler, Taibi 34
Köhler, Dorothee 180

L lack of time 21
lateral thinking 155, 156
leadership 17–18, 22, 29, 79
– agile 82, 84, 102
– rotating 36
– Situational Leadership 99
– tools 92
listening 44, 77, 91, 113–114, 129, 141

M management 16, 26, 28
– career path 84
– peer 60
– practice 92, 144
– situations 63
– strategic 15, 29
– tasks 15
Marinetti, Filippo 167
Marquard, Odo 167
Maslow, Abraham 99–100
memory, not reliable 162
mentoring 83, 94
middle crunch *see* sandwich position
mirroring 118–119
motivation 100
Murray, Bill 164

N NASA 34
needs 137
– mental/emotional 45, 132–133
– unmet 40
neuroscience 56

O opportunism 92

Osborn Checklist 144, 155
Osborn, Alex f. 144, 155
Oshry, Barry 21–22, 55, 154
overload 21, 22, 28–29
overtaxed *see* overload

P past
– acknowledging the 159, 171–173
– fixation on 161, 164
Persister (PCM) 34–35, 37, 40, 43, 75–76, 105, 128–129
personality types 34–36, 44, 46, 129
perspective, change of 17–18, 71, 155, 157
power games 52
present, acknowledging the 171–172
Probing 123
problem-solving 67–68, 165
– creative 155
– process 159
– three directions 159
Process Communication Model (PCM) 34, 40, 45, 51, 55, 75, 105, 124, 129, 139
projections 122, 124
Promoter (PCM) 34–35, 105
provocative question 70
psychotherapy 83–84
Push and Pull 88

Q questioning techniques 143, 150, 157
questions
– crazy 153
– open 122–124, 128, 143–145
– provocative 71
– solutions in disguise 113

R rapport 31, 38, 59, 92, 114, 118–119, 124, 165, 170
reality (GROW) 144
reality check 128, 146, 151, 155
Rebel (PCM) 34–35
recognition 40
reflex 21, 161
– predictable reflex response 21
relationships 40, 71
resources 89, 94, 108, 150
– mobilize 157
responsibility 17–18, 22
room to maneuver 29, 134

S sandwich position 55, 62
scaling questions 144, 149–151, 157
self-confidence 98, 100, 105
self-determination 134
self-help 77

Index

- helping people help themselves 77–79, 82–83, 93–95, 100–101, 108, 139
self-reflection 40, 45
Shakespeare, William 123
slider principle 88
small steps 60, 67, 150
small talk 51–52, 75, 87, 119
Socrates 143
solution energy 70, 129, 134, 139, 155
solution vision 165
strategy 17, 89
strategy dilemma 17
stress 22, 40
- response 34
stress patterns 21–22, 39, 41, 55, 62, 128–129
structures 89
success 33, 144–145
systemic triangle 89, 92

T tacit assumptions 114, 123–124
teaching 82–84
Thinker (PCM) 34–35, 40–41, 43–44, 55, 75, 105

Three-step technique 137–138
time, lack of 15, 29
TO-GROW model 144–147, 157
Tolstoy, Leo 161, 164
top performer 98, 101, 106, 138
training 82–83
transfer skills 102
trust 50–51, 71, 109, 117–118, 124, 128, 156–157

U uncertainty 17–18

V values 130, 139
visualization 150
volatility 17–18
VUCA 17–19, 22, 26, 28–29, 33

W war for talent 25
Whitmore, John 144

Y younger version *see* inner child

Z Zoll, Jörg Achim 180